A FEW SWEET HOURS
A PAGEANT OF POETRY

The door to
Beauty is
The soul;
The poet
Holds the
Key

POET LAUREATE

II

A Few Sweet Hours

· A Pageant of Poetry ·

Is A Presentation Of

Inspirational Selections
Country Verse & Lyrics
Fun & Fantasy
and
Verses Of The Heart

From The Works Of

POET/HUMORIST

William Spicer

ILLUSTRATED & HANDPENNED
IN CALLIGRAPHIC CONCEPT BY

Edith Reed

In Memory
of
Erling Reed

v

FOREWORD

Not only was William Spicer an accomplished poet, but he loved to entertain and was an actor in his own right. Reciting from his abundant repertoire of poems and homespun yarns, many in country verse, his poetry recitals delighted audiences and often brought them to their feet in standing ovation. It is in this spirit of theatrical flamboyance that his work is presented here in the concept of a pageant.

"Play on words" was another of Mr. Spicer's loves and talents. It might be said that he had a gift for "*PUN* tificating." He saw comedy in situations created by the double meaning of words and with a twinkle of humor, he set them to rhyme. His "*HAM* onyms" were his hamming of homonyms, and are typical of his amusing and clever word play.

He loved to write poetry, taught it in public schools, authored a newspaper column and charmed people from all walks of life with his recitals. His paperback poetry book, *LYRICAL, SATIRICAL & SLIGHTLY HYSTERICAL,* was published in 1979. He was a lover of books and his personal library contained over a thousand volumes on an extensive range of subjects. He was an avid sports fan, respected winning coaches and was himself, a spirited competitor.

By profession, he was a piano and accordion teacher and it was this talent and his love of music that brought him and his students many honors. However, nearest to his heart was his desire to impress on young people the many benefits of clean living and purposeful lives and to motivate them to strive for personal accomplishment and excellence. In his own words, *"the best is yet to be done."*

During the 1950's and 60's, he coached his accordion soloists and bands to many First and Second Place Honors in the National Accordion Competitions in Chicago, Illinois and New York City. They won State Championships in Minnesota and repeatedly in Florida. He was considered a musical genius by many. Strangely enough, he played no musical instrument himself.

William Spicer was a farm boy, born September 2, 1914 in Sparta, Michigan, and some of his poems relate to farm life in the early twenties.

As a teenager, he lived in Seattle, Washington, graduating in 1934 from West Seattle High School. His career took him to the Midwest, where he was graduated from Graceland College and Millikin University. He was the father of three children, Marilyn Burgess of Hawaii, Michael Spicer and Ramona Hartnett of Orlando, Florida. He has one grandchild, Duke Burgess of Hawaii.

Mr. Spicer was gifted with a vivid imagination and a pleasant sense of humor. He had a searching mind and an active and varied life. His light-hearted writings can be enjoyed by young and old alike and his more serious selections are thought-provoking--sometimes challenging--but his casual style makes easy reading for all ages.

Mr. Spicer was inspired to write abundantly on an exceptionally wide range of subjects and circumstances. Because of his quest for spiritual answers, he wrote, among others, such works as THE QUESTION OF ETERNAL LIFE. A church, for an anniversary celebration, engaged him to write THE NEW SONG. He often wrote to explain a principle, sometimes through dialogue.

Many of his writings commemorate events that touched his own life, such as THE NUMBER ONE PRO, written when his daughter, Ramona Hartnett, a former Mrs. Florida, became a Gold Medalist in 1990 as a member of the trio that won the Reebok World Championship in Aerobics.

THE BALLAD OF THE BUM sprang from his imagination, based upon his experiences when he rode the rails during the Great Depression. Likewise, Country Verse poems reflect folklife's colloquial dialogue that once existed in many remote areas of our country.

AMERICAN HERITAGE records family history, one involving a notorious bank robber, and other selections, such as WHEN I WAS JES' A KID, BOOK OF DREAMS, HIDDEN TREASURE and others, mark the passing of the "horse and buggy" era.

While the poetry presented here includes many familiar early favorites, much of it is Mr. Spicer's final work. This book was in constant revision in an effort to assure that readers could enjoy the best of Mr. Spicer's literary treasures.

My friendship with William Spicer was established in high school and spanned more than half a century. But consideration of a joint effort in producing a book first emerged as I, at age 66, inspired by KEN BROWN's CALLIGRAPHY HANDBOOK, pursued my new retirement hobby of letterforms. After I had "done my thing" with some of Mr.Spicer's poems, his response was, "If you're going to that much work, the book should really be a publication."

Time passed. I became more involved. Then, with considerable apprehension, I began the book, A FEW SWEET HOURS, in January, 1984, while intensifying my study of letterforms and searching desperately for guidance in organizing the work of this prolific poet.

Because I was unable to find a mentor who had done a similar project, the ensuing eight years were, by necessity, a hard-working period of experimenting and "learning by doing" and "re-doing". During this time, the need for color and illustration emerged and beginning in 1988, it was a matter of more "trial and error" experimenting as I developed art and drawing through the "self-taught" approach.

This book is not intended as an exemplar, but rather as a medium for sharing A FEW SWEET HOURS with others, for I am strictly a hobbyist, never having done a manuscript of any kind for remuneration. While such teachers as Dewey Henderson of WRITE ON CALLIGRAPHERS OF EDMONDS, Denys Taipale-Knight and Stanley Knight at the Farmhouse, Marc Drogin at a conference, all inspired me to work tirelessly for rhythmical cadence and letterform perfection, time ran out, occasionally causing important objectives to be compromised for the sake of including the poem.

Mr. Spicer's demise at his Florida residence on December 2, 1991, just as this book was nearing publication, was a devastating development.With the encouragement and support of my husband of 54 years, Erling Reed, I finished the book in April, 1992. Efforts to publish at that time were set aside as illness befell my husband. He was my number one priority. He died on May 2, 1995.

My interest in publishing A FEW SWEET HOURS was rekindled in 1996 when I came upon some William Spicer poems that I felt should be included in the book. I began preparing them, never dreaming how difficult this would be, for my hands will no longer do the work that once brought me so much joy. But finally, the project is completed and some of the best of Mr. Spicer's work is integrated into this book.

As I write these closing words, I am celebrating my 79th birthday. How good life has been to allow me to see this book to publication! And how important! Important because....

A FEW SWEET HOURS is more than A Pageant of Poetry. In a unique way it captures and preserves for posterity the values and life-style of a passing generation.Some of Mr.Spicer's works were created when he was a Senior, thus they reflect on a time of life familiar to many readers in the so-called Golden Years. He will be remembered for his exceptional love of challenge and his positive winning attitude as well as his sense of humor, gift of inspiring words and remarkable musical talent.

To those who have had no previous interest in poetry or lyrical text, may you discover that it can be entertaining, that it can be fun!

And now, dear reader-audience, may you find joy and respite in A FEW SWEET HOURS: A Pageant Of Poetry as William Spicer's final performance leaves us all the legacy of a truly All-American poet, *and may each of you find your own highest potential in the dawn of a great tomorrow!*

Edith Jorgensen Reed
May, 1997

In Thanks

This book would not be complete without a word of thanks to JAMES KING for his editorial guidance and support in the final stages of bringing this book to completion. to his wife, BETTY, for her continuing and inspiring enthusiasm for calligraphy. to MARY DANIELSON for her technical help. to our daughter, JANICE LOGG for problem-solving. to our sons, FREDRIC and RICHARD REED for specialized assistance. to all my family for encouragement and especially to my late husband of fifty-four years, ERLING REED for his ever-pleasant spirit of co-operation and his life-long example of untiring perseverance. A heart-felt thanks to all

Edith Reed

The Bequest

On Behalf of
the poet and the scribe, one of
the motivating purposes of producing this
book was to preserve the work herein
for our respective children and their
families.
In That Context

"A FEW SWEET HOURS: A Pageant of Poetry"
is endowed to the following:

William Spicer's family: To his daughter,
Marilyn, and her husband, Roy Burgess,
and their son, Duke; to Mr. Spicer's
daughter, Ramona, and husband, Pat Hartnett
and to Mr. Spicer's son, Michael.

Edith Reed's family: To our daughter,
Janice Logg; our son, Fredric and his wife,
Tana, and their children, Darby and Trevor;
our son, Richard, and his wife, Patricia,
and their sons, Ryan and Jason. In memory
of Erling Reed.

In Tribute
TO THE STATES

From the Majestic glaciers of ALASKA to the fragile fauna of FLORIDA, as unique and varied as the panoramic collage of the land are the cultural heritages and lifestyles of the people in this kaleidoscope of fifty states that are one nation

THE UNITED STATES OF AMERICA

Equally diverse are the impressions and inspirations,

that take expression in these poems written in memory of some of the states.

XVI

DEDICATED TO POETRY LOVERS
Everywhere

Especially to those
who
delight in rhythmic verse and
poetic scenarios, perhaps
with a message or
a touch of humor,
and to those as well
who love
calligraphic perceptions
and the art of
Letterforms

XVIII

The Soul-Stirring
MAGIC OF POETRY

Composers set it to music for listening pleasure.
Painters translate it into pictures.
The contemporary scribe gives it

Calligraphic Visualization

in yet another expression inspired
by the beauty of the
rhythmic verse.

EDITH REED

XIX

xx

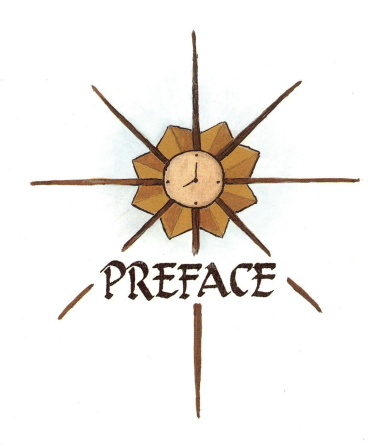

PREFACE

THE DOOR TO BEAUTY

I chanced upon two artists painting
in their chosen way.
While one, a poet, in his musing,
Penned a roundelay
The other captured tone in paint.
They both had such a flair
And style I hardly dared to breathe.
My senses feasted there.

XXII

I thought, which one of these is greatest,
He who paints in word
Or he with brush and pallette? Surely
Each is moved and spurred
By his own favorite muse or god
To reach the highest crest--
But still my mind kept asking, which
Is counted best?

I sought the counsel of a sage
Whose tools were brush and script.
A poet-painter, one who drank
Where others only sipped.
"Your quest," he said, "is one of worth,
So hear the words I speak.
Suppose your artists both aspire
To paint a mountain peak.
While one will seek the mountain out,
Content with weather's whim,
The other waits, Mohammed-like;
The mountain comes to him."

I chanced upon two artists painting
In their chosen way.
I asked them, "Who is greatest here?"
I heard the painter say:
"I hold a mirror up to nature,
Mine is what I see.
The door to beauty is the soul;
The poet holds the key."

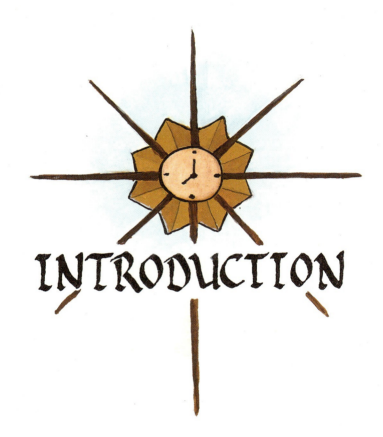

INTRODUCTION

A Few Sweet Hours

How often I, in memory,
Have quit the busy day
To clasp a lingering, childhood scene!
The life-worn mold of clay
Can hardly hold the spirit back
When bygone days reach up
And gently touch the hand of time.
It's then the waiting cup
Is filled to overflowing. Yes,
It's then my eye beholds
The treasured scenes of yesteryear:

Another life unfolds . . .

How strange!

These pictures of the past
Seem carved in walls of stone,
While recent and far grander scenes
Have taken wing. Alone
I sit and muse upon a life
No longer mine. And yet,
How kind the years have been to save
A few sweet hours, and let
Me taste their goodness once again -

I walk along the shore
Of living's past. I am content
To dream, and ask no more.

WILLIAM SPICER

XXVII

A Few Sweet Hours

• A Pageant of Poetry •

By

William Spicer
POET • HUMORIST

Edith Reed
SCRIBE • ILLUSTRATOR

Program

A FEW SWEET HOURS

A Pageant of Poetry

By William Spicer

PRESENTED BY EDITH REED

1996

Seattle, Washington
Orlando, Florida

P·R·E·S·E·N·T·E·D
IN SIX PARTS

— PRESENTATION —

Part I
THE BOUNTY OF LIFE
Yesteryears · Nature · Dreams

◆

Part II
VIGNETTES OF YOUTH
Love · Believing

◆

Part III
TIDES OF CHALLENGE
Courage · Patriotism

◆

Part IV
MOODS OF REFLECTION
Sorrow · Memories · Live Now

◆

Part V
POETRY JUST FOR FUN
Country Verse & Lyrics,
Clowning · "HAMonyms" · Satire

◆

Part VI
FINALE
The Dawn Of Tomorrow

A Few Sweet Hours

· A Pageant of Poetry ·

By William Spicer

ORDER OF PRESENTATION

Part I

THE BOUNTY OF LIFE

INTRODUCTORY SCROLL
PRESENTATION OF POET
FOLIO SEQUENCE

FOLIO ONE

The Spirit of YESTERYEARS
& The Endearments

FOLIO TWO

The Wonderment of NATURE & Her Masterpieces

—ANIMATED INTERLUDE—

FOLIO THREE

The Enchantment of DREAMS & Fantasies

Part II

VIGNETTES OF YOUTH

SCROLL OF FOLIOS
POET IN RECITATION
FOLIO SEQUENCE
FOLIO FOUR

The Joy & Ecstacy of LOVE → The Torch & The Tears,

FOLIO FIVE

The Enrichment of BELIEVING & The Fulfillment

— FULFILLMENT —

THE TIDES OF CHALLENGE

SCROLL OF FOLIOS
POET
FOLIO SEQUENCE

FOLIO SIX

The Inspiration of COURAGE
& The Commitment to Striving

FOLIO SEVEN

The Pride of PATRIOTISM
& Dedication To Freedom & Peace

INTERMISSION

Part IV

MOODS OF REFLECTION
SCROLL OF FOLIOS
POET
FOLIO SEQUENCE

FOLIO EIGHT

The Melancholy of SORROW
& The Hand of Fate

— ▾ ▾ ▾ —

(PART IV)
CONTINUED

FOLIO NINE

The Nostalgia of MEMORIES
& The Pain of Progress

—THE PAIN OF PROGRESS—

FOLIO TEN

About Today... Take Time to LIVE
—Now

Part V

POETRY JUST FOR FUN

SCROLL OF FOLIOS
POET
FOLIO SEQUENCE
FOLIO ELEVEN

The Twinkle & Good Humor of
COUNTRY VERSE & LYRICS

— ▼ ▼ ▼ —

Part VI

FINALE

SCROLL OF FOLIOS
POET
FOLIO SEQUENCE

FOLIO FOURTEEN

The Dawn of TOMORROW

THE VERSE OF LIFE
— FINALE —
Epilogue

The Lights Are Dimmed

It's Curtain Time

Part I

THE BOUNTY OF LIFE

Folio Sequence

FOLIO ONE

YESTERYEARS

FOLIO TWO

NATURE

FOLIO THREE

DREAMS

FOLIO ONE
YESTERYEARS

FOLIO ONE

YESTERYEARS

AMERICAN HERITAGE
GRANDMA'S
       HARPSICHORD
TWO TINY FEET
A SONG FOR MICHAEL

AMERICAN HERITAGE

FATHER WAS A LOGGER, OLD AT TWELVE,
A MEMBER OF THE ROUGH AND HARDY SET
THAT PIKED AND DOGGED
THE STANDS OF DIAMOND TIMBER
NORTH AND WEST AS FAR AS THEY COULD GET.

A WAR? WHAT WAR? YOU SAY BETWEEN THE STATES?
A DONKEY TAKE THE PLACE OF HORSE? A THING
THAT RUNS BY STEAM?
                    LET'S HAUL OUT WHAT WE HAVE;
FIRST SNOW THAT FALLS
WE'RE STUCK OUT HERE TILL SPRING.

KANSAS WAS A DIFFERENT KIND OF WORLD.

MY MOTHER, OLDEST OF THE EIGHT, WAS STILL
A CHILD WHEN LIGHTNING STRUCK AND TOOK HER FATHER.
WHO, OUT THERE, WOULD CHALLENGE FATE? THE WILL
OF GOD? PERHAPS...THE HOUSE OF SOD NOT BIG
ENOUGH FOR TEN.
BUT CHANCE NOR JESSE JAMES
COULD CARE WHO DIED OR HOW.

                    THE LITTLE LIFE
THAT STRUGGLED THERE WITHOUT COMPLAINT OR CLAIMS
WAS HOW IT WAS. AND SHE, TOO YOUNG TO YEARN,
WAS OLD ENOUGH TO EARN UNBUTTERED BREAD
AND WATCH THE PLUNDERED TOWN OF LAWRENCE BURN.

I THANK THEM BOTH, WHEREVER THEY MAY BE,
WHO, HAVING LITTLE, GAVE SO MUCH TO ME.

29

GRANDMA'S HARPSICHORD

My grandma had a spacious house,
At least it seemed that way to me.
I went there as a child and saw
So many charming things as she
Would take me by the hand and show
Me all around.

Each room was very
Special: kitchen with its massive
Iron stove with oven where she
Baked the bread and mincemeat pie
The bedroom with a fireplace
Across one end, the maple walls .
And high brass bed with spread of lace.

My favorite was the music room.
Van Dyck's Pieta on the wall
Above my grandma's harpsichord,
A smoking stand—as I recall,
I thought it strange that no one smoked—
A roll-top desk where Grandpa sat
Whenever Grandma played for him,

Until the day....Then after that
His chair was mine to use when she
Would play.

Whatever pleasures be
My lot in life, I'll never know
The sweet peace I knew when she,
With loving fingers, touched the keys.
"Our Amadeus," she would say.
And all the past would live. And I
Could want no more than
Hear her play.

Time has wrapped his arms around
Those joys with quiet, gentle grace.
And when the evening casts its spell,
And all is still, there is a trace
Of Mozart in the air. I close
My eyes and see a smoking stand,
A roll-top desk where Grandpa sits,
And then, my grandma
Takes my hand.

I think with sadness of the day
Those little feet will go away...

Excerpt: TWO TINY FEET
Wm Spicer

TWO TINY FEET

I kiss two tiny, little feet,
So soft and smooth, so warm and sweet,
That found their way from beneath the clothes—
Two tiny feet, ten tiny toes.

Two tiny feet; too tiny still
To chase the shadows on the hill,
Or make me start to hear a pair
Of little shoes upon the stair.

I think with sadness of the day
Those little feet will go away,
To fill some other home with care,
To tread upon some other stair.

I kiss two tiny, little feet,
So soft and smooth, so warm and sweet;
I tuck them back beneath the clothes—
Two tiny feet, ten tiny toes.

A SONG FOR MICHAEL

The angels must have done it,
 No mortal could have wrought
This fragile rhapsody
 Of love and trust and need.

No bold sophistication,
 A plain and simple soul
Who has no want or care
 For scheming, plot or creed.

He takes his lot for granted,
 And all so unaware
That where perfection is
 There is no right or wrong.

What errant act of nature,
 What careless twist of fate
Or karmic dictum ever
 Sang so sweet a song?

The angels must have done it.

The angels must have done it. No mortal could have wrought
This fragile rhapsody of love and trust and need.

Excerpt: A SONG FOR MICHAEL
Wm. Spicer.

FOLIO TWO
NATURE

THE WONDERMENT OF
NATURE &
HER MASTERPIECES

FOLIO TWO

NATURE

THE WINDING ROAD
BIG SKY COUNTRY
FLORIDA IS...
TIME'S EXTRAVAGANZA
GOD'S MASTERPIECE
PRELUDE TO WINTER
BY REQUEST
NATURE'S BEQUEST

—ANIMATED INTERLUDE—

A FLOWER SETTLES
    THE QUESTION
THE BEE AND THE ROACH
FOOD FOR THOUGHT

THE WINDING ROAD

I LIKE TO DRIVE A WINDING ROAD
WITH TREES AND ROCKS AND HILLS,
AND LAKES REFLECTING
SUMMER CLOUDS;
A PLACE WHERE NATURE SPILLS
HER BEAUTY CARELESSLY FOR HIM
WHO HAS A MIND TO SEE
WHAT OTHERS TAKE FOR GRANTED, LIKE
A ROCK, A HILL OR TREE.

I LIKE TO THINK THAT GOD INTENDED
WE SHOULD TAKE THE TIME
TO NOTICE HOW HE WROUGHT IT—
WITH SUCH AN UNOBTRUSIVE RHYME—
THE FOLD OF GOLD
AND GREEN ALL BLENDED
TRUE TO NATURE'S ART,
AND EACH STONE CAST
AS THOUGH TO PLAY
A VERY SPECIAL PART;
TO NOTICE HOW THE HILLS
WERE PLACED
A BACKDROP FOR THE SCENE,
WITH LAKE IN FRONT
AND WILLOWS GROWING
ON THE BANKS BETWEEN.

THE SUPER HIGHWAY
HAS A PLACE
WITH ALL ITS MODERN FRILLS,
BUT I WILL TAKE A WINDING ROAD
WITH TREES AND ROCKS AND HILLS.

39

BIG SKY COUNTRY

Out where the sky is big and clear,
 Where a man can breathe,
  And the white-tailed deer
 Come down from the timber without a fear,
  Whether their season is in or out...

Out where the rancher owns a spread,
 Where the land is his,
  And he earns his bread;
 If he doesn't show, it's a cinch hes dead
  Or up at the cataract catching trout...

Out where the mountains rake the skies,
 Where the north wind blows
  And the south wind sighs;
 You've only to be there to realize
  Some things a life shouldn't be without.

Montana, you know, I'm talking about.

FLORIDA IS . . . .

A pasture stretched from shore to shore,
    A cameo of jade;
A montage made of silly tales
    Etched in errant shade;
A fairyland of sun and sand
    Framed in azure blue;
And all of nature's floral magic
    Marshalled for review;

Lakes and rivers; everglades;
    Ranches, groves and keys;
Wind enough to test a sail;
    Moss-draped cypress trees;
A silvery, sand dune bordered beach
    Where people play and laugh;
A world of places made to carve
    A worry's epitaph;
A feathered, singing plagiarist;
    A wealth of fitful showers;
A rare perfume of citrus bloom;
    Tropic trees and flowers;
A thousand aves answered here;
    Ours, hers and his;
All the things that one could want...
    That's what Florida is.

41

Time's Extravaganza

The sun is waiting in the wing,
    Kismetic, sure and steady;
The mountain backdrop in its place,
    The songbirds tuned and ready.

The twinkling house-lights, dimmed, await
    The opening act of birth.
The curtain rises on a day —
    The greatest show on earth.

God's Masterpiece

Words fall short
And praise is empty;
Sky and sea and sod
Are molded by Infinity-
A Masterpiece of God.

There is a land, 'The Last Frontier,'
The nation's golden crest,
Where even beauty acquiesces;
Grandeur at its best.
A land like something never dreamed,
With peaks that sweep the sky,
Their giant gorges crammed with ice,
And winds that sing and sigh.
The brave and bold have sought her treasure;
Dreamers, gaunt and lean,
Have sluiced her streams and trapped her trails,
For most untouched, unseen.

Her sea is calling: "Come and dare
To share your strength with mine;
How soon you'll see there's more to me
Than waves of icy brine.
My shores are miles of paradise

Words fall short and

PRAISE is empty.

Sky and sea and sod
Are molded by Infinity—
A Masterpiece of

GOD

EXCERPT: GOD'S MASTERPIECE
Wm Spicer

44

Without the spoil and stains
Of man. Still welcome those who seek
A place where Nature reigns.
There's coves and narrows, inlets, capes:
No fences here, or sign
Where man has placed his 'Private' stamp;
"These shares are God's and mine."

A beauty-bonus waits for those
Who come with eyes for sights;
The magic wonder of the skies,
A show called 'Northern Lights.'
There's none can stage it, or predict
What kind of show 'twill be.
No ticket lines or 'Sold Out' signs:
The 'Northern Lights' is free.

So dream a dream of midnight sun,
And dream of seas and sails,
Yes, dream of tides and rocks and shores
And sunsets, glaciers, gales.
It's waiting there for you to come;
No, not the traps or gold,
The beauty, silence, majesty,
More dear a thousand-fold.

PRELUDE TO WINTER

I could tell by the way the cat-tails
    alongside the bank
       were bent
and the way the water
    had pounded the rock
       that whatever remained of the living
        was in for a freeze.

But nature wouldn't strike without warning
    the season's clock
      the foliage
       had pointed its hands
        to yellow and red
and the maple
    as bare as a baby
       stood with its arms outstretched
       and waited

The setting was usually moving with life
  but

        except for a lingering line of geese
            that was etched

                on a low-hanging cloud
it was more like
    a seasonal wake

Had I not seen it all acted out
    many times in the past
        I would wonder
            who had staged such a show
I would probably ask
    who had written the script
        and just where he had found
            such a cast

BY REQUEST

Had I the strength, had I the time
  I'd find a mountain I could climb.
      I wouldn't take the common trail
  Or try where stronger men might fail,
  But go where none has ever been
      Save God. Perhaps a patch of green
      Hedged about by birch would fit
  My mood. And there I'd dream a bit.

I guess by mountain climbing measure
  I'm attracted more to leisure.
      Leastwise when I reach the top
  It won't have been without a stop.
  And when I think back down the trail
      My mind will see behind the veil
      To where the real beauty lies.
  If we could only realize
  That nature always hides her best
      And shows it only by request!

NATURE

Always hides her best
& shows
it only
by Request

~Excerpt: BY REQUEST
~Wm Spicer

NATURE'S BEQUEST

The rose has withered on the stem.
The golden clusters of the vine
Have fallen to the earth. The songs
That echoed through the oak and pine
Have died upon the thrush's throat.

How often, touched with morning dew,
The petalled jewel moved a heart
Where tongue had failed. What skill of man
Can bear one drop of wine, or art
Reflect the songbird's slightest note?

All nature leaves a wondrous touch;
Would God that we could leave as much.

—ANIMATED INTERLUDE—

I'D NEVER heard

a flower speak

But this one did I swear.

And what she said has had effect

on everything I wear —

Excerpt: A FLOWER SETTLES
THE QUESTION

Wm. Spicer

52

A FLOWER SETTLES The Question

I'd heard it said so many times,
    "You don't wear blue with green."
That I was careful when I dressed
    Those colors not be seen.

I chanced, along a mountain trail
    -imagine my surprise-,
To find a flower green and blue
    Before my very eyes.
I said, "You naughty little plant,
    How dare you show your face?
The colors you so boldly flaunt
    Are bound to bring disgrace."
I must confess, upon reflection,
    Just a touch of shame
For having been so harsh with her
    And quick to place the blame.
I'd never heard a flower speak
    But this one did I swear.
And what she said has had effect
    On everything I wear.

My shirt is blue, my jacket green;
    Her words have so impressed me.
"You'll have to place the blame on God
    For He's the one who dressed me."

THE BEE AND THE ROACH

Said Mr. Roach to Mrs. Bee,
    "My friend, how do you do?
I've noticed with some interest
    How fortune smiles on you.

"You fly about the posey patch
    Without a fear or care
As though our enemy, the man,
    Would never find you there

"What magic charm do you possess
    That man would hunt me out
And treat me like a common pest
    And let you fly about?"

Said Mrs. Bee to Mr. Roach,
    "Perhaps it's time you knew

Why man treats me so kindly while
    He's always after you.

"A rule exists among the living,
    And it's fair and true;
It's made for man, it's made for woman
    And for bugs like you.

"It's called the Law of Compensation:
    Those who give shall get,
But those who give not of themselves
    Are found to be in debt.

"The blossom gives me of her nectar,
    I give man my honey,
He may send a needy friend
    A gift of clothes or money.

"You, Sir Roach, have given nothing,
    So you pay your debt
By being hunted like a thief;
    You can't escape the net.

"Some have tried, to no avail;
    The law is sure and true.
Your days are numbered, Mr. Roach,
    And so I say, 'adieu'."

FOOD
FOR
THOUGHT

One day while I was busy digging
  IN MY GARDEN SPOT
  I WITNESSED SOMETHING I MUST SHARE
  ALTHOUGH I'D RATHER NOT.
  I SAY I'D RATHER NOT BECAUSE,
  YOU SEE I CAN'T CONFIRM,
  WITH RATIONALITY, THAT I
  WAS TALKING WITH A WORM.

But there I stood with spade in hand
  WHEN FROM BENEATH A SOD
  THIS WRINKLED CREATURE WIGGLED OUT
  WITH JUST THE SLIGHTEST NOD.
  "I SAY," SAID HE, "WE HAVEN'T MET

BUT WOULD YOU BE SO KIND
AS TELL ME WHY YOU'RE DIGGING HERE
AND WHAT YOU HOPE TO FIND?"

I didn't wish to make an issue
OR PUT ON AN AIR
BUT WHAT I DO WITH MY OWN GROUND
IS STRICTLY MY AFFAIR.
SO, WITH A SMILE, I SAID TO HIM,
"MY FRIEND, I SEE NO NEED
TO ANSWER HOW I USE THE LAND
THAT'S MINE BY RIGHT OF DEED."

"By right of deed, indeed," he said,
"NO DOUBT A SOUND EXPRESSION;
I'VE LIVED HERE A MILLION YEARS
AND OWN IT BY POSSESSION."
'WELL, WHAT IF I SHOULD TAKE MY SPADE
AND CHOP YOU RIGHT IN TWO?"
"I'D GROW ANOTHER HALF," HE SAID,
AND THEN HE ASKED, "COULD YOU?"

I thought, what ever is the purpose
OF THIS WIGGLY WORM
WHO SEEMS TO HAVE NO OTHER USE
THAN JUST TO TWIST AND SQUIRM
I SMILED, "HERE COMES A HUNGRY JAY,
I FEAR YOU'LL SOON BE DEAD."
"YOU SILLY MAN, THAT'S WHY I'M HERE.
WHAT'S YOUR EXCUSE?" HE SAID.

I sat upon a rock and watched.
I WONDERED, COULD IT BE
THAT GOD, UPON HIS THRONE OF GRACE,
IS LIKEWISE WATCHING ME.

FOLIO THREE
DREAMS

The Enchantment of DREAMS & Fantasies

FOLIO THREE

DREAMS

I'LL TAKE A DREAM
THE DREAMER
CRY OF THE DREAMER
BE CAREFUL
    WHAT YOU DREAM

I'll Take A Dream

I'll take a lazy mountain stream
    Where happy waters dance and gleam
    In early morning sun
    As though they've naught to do but play
    And while the carefree hours away
    Until the day is done.

I'll dream of scaling mountain walls
    And walking down Valhalla halls
    Where eagle stalls and floats
    Around a silent mountain peak
    Where only nature dares to speak
    Or sing her echoed notes.

Be yours the busy city life;
    Reality, a routine, rife
    With all its gaud and shine,
    The tinseled trappings of esteem.
    Be yours to labor and to scheme —
    I'll take a dream for mine.

THE DREAMER

They call me dreamer because my head
    is always in a cloud.
I guess it's true I look for things
    I've never been allowed.
Fame and wealth have passed me by,
    this life's not what it's deemed.
But don't I have a little more
    than if I'd never dreamed?

IT'S TRUE THAT COLD REALITY
    HAS STRUCK A FATEFUL BLOW,
FOR WHERE MY STATELY CASTLE STOOD
    THERE'S JUST A BUNGALOW.
THE KNIGHT IN DAZZLING COAT OF MAIL
    WAS JUST A BIT EXTREME.
HOW ELSE COULD I HAVE HAD SO MUCH
    EXCEPT IT BE A DREAM?

WHERE OTHER LOSS WOULD CAUSE DESPAIR,
    MY HOPE IS NEVER BLIGHTED
BECAUSE I HOLD DEVALUED DREAMS
    OR FIND MY FANCY SLIGHTED.
IF ALL MY DREAMS ARE DREAMED IN VAIN,
    MY SPIRIT NEVER SMOTHERS;
I SIMPLY LAY THOSE DREAMS ASIDE
    AND DREAM MYSELF SOME OTHERS.

CRY OF THE DREAMER

I WOULD KNOW THE LUXURY
OF SEEING THINGS I NEVER SEE
EXCEPT IN DREAMS; AND I WOULD SENSE
A SHARE OF STRIVING'S RECOMPENSE.
IT'S NOT ENOUGH TO DREAM THE DREAM
THAT PLAGUES ME FROM MY YOUTH, THE THEME
THAT SOMEHOW LINGERS THROUGH THE YEARS,
BLAZES, FADES AND REAPPEARS.

64

I WOULD LIVE AND FEEL THE DREAM,
THE SEA-SET SAILS AND WINDS THAT SCREAM,
THE REARING "STEED" AGAINST THE SKY,
THE PLUNGE, THE SPRAY, THE SEA-GULL'S CRY,
A FOAM-LACED LINE AGAINST THE GREEN,
A FALL, A CLIFF, A COVE BETWEEN,
A CHALLENGE MET, A STRUGGLE WON,
AN ANCHORAGE WHEN DAY IS DONE.

I WOULD KNOW THE QUIET HUSH
OF CLOSING DAY AND SEE THE BLUSH
OF FADING SUN, A GENTLE SEA,
AUTUMN'S GOLD IN HARMONY,
MOUNTAINS CLAD IN WINTER CLOTHES,
SPRINGTIME'S DEW AND SUMMER'S ROSE...
ALL THE THINGS I LONG TO SEE,
WELLED UP HERE INSIDE OF ME.

I SIGH AND SEE BEYOND THIS CAGE—
THIS GRAND FACADE, THIS POTTING STAGE—
A TREASURED DREAM THAT TIME AND CARE
HAVE CLAIMED BECAUSE I DID NOT DARE.
I DID NOT DARE TO CLAIM MY OWN,
TO HARVEST WHERE THE GODS HAVE SOWN;
I COULD NOT SEE THE DEVIL'S SCHEME
UNTIL TOO LATE...AND SO, I DREAM.

BE CAREFUL WHAT YOU DREAM

Be careful what you dream about,
　　A dream is often truth
That hasn't yet been realized.
　　A maiden, in her youth,
Had dreamed of having wealthy prince;
　　A sheik was good as any.
Her dream came true but she wants out
　　For she's just one of many.

Be careful what you wish because
　　Your wishes have a way
Of taking on reality.
　　I heard a fellow say,
"I sure would like to have a wife."
　　It wasn't very long
He got his wish, and now he sings
　　A different kind of song.

I wouldn't say you shouldn't dream
　　Or never make a wish.
The one who does not dream of casting
　　Never catches fish.
Don't be alarmed though, once you dream,
　　If fortune sees you get it.
Don't curse the clock that wakens you
　　If you're the one who set it.

66

DON'T BE
ALARMED if though
Once you dream
if fortune sees
you get it,

don't curse the clock that wakens you,
if you're the one who set it.

Excerpt: BE CAREFUL WHAT YOU DREAM
Wm. Spicer

Part II

VIGNETTES OF YOUTH

Folio Sequence

FOLIO FOUR
LOVE

FOLIO FIVE
BELIEVING

FOLIO FOUR
LOVE

The Joy & Ecstacy of
LOVE →...
The Torch of Tears

FOLIO FOUR

LOVE

THAT'S WHAT IT'S LIKE
         TO BE IN LOVE
OUT OF SEASON
THE FIRST OF EVERYTHING
YOU
LOVE'S DEFINITION
IF I HAD MY WAY
ANNIVERSARY THOUGHT
A SONG OF PARTING
BETRAYED
TO A LOST LOVE

THAT'S WHAT IT'S LIKE·
T' BE IN LOVE

I'm UPSIDE down an' INSIDE out;
I don't KNOW what it's ALL about;
   THAT'S WHAT IT'S LIKE T' BE IN LOVE.

I'm SCARED t' go out on the STREET,
THEY say I WALK with TWO LEFT FEET;
   THAT'S WHAT IT'S LIKE T' BE IN LOVE.

I SIT UP WHEN the SUN goes DOWN,
My DAYS an' NIGHTS are TURNED around;
   I don't KNOW DOWN BELOW FROM UP ABOVE.

I should be WORKIN' makin' BREAD.
BuT here I AM at home instead;
   THAT'S WHAT IT'S LIKE T' BE IN LOVE.

I MOW the DRIVE an' SWEEP the LAWN,
I lock the DOOR BEFORE I've GONE,
I WIND the CAT an FEED the CLOCK;
An TURN on BACH INSTEAD of ROCK;
   THAT'S WHAT IT'S LIKE T' BE IN LOVE.

OUT OF SEASON

She was sweet and twenty-three
    And I was sixty-two.
I held her hand and said "Goodnight."
    What else was I to do?
I would have held her in my arms
    But that would never do,
For she was twenty-three
    While I was sixty-two.

I met her at the Mardi Gras.
    At Leon's French Chateau.
She asked if I would drink with her;
    Could I have answered "NO"?
She drank a glass of Vin Rosé;
    I drank a Mountain Dew
For she was only twenty-three
    While I was sixty-two.

She was sweet and twenty-three
    With all that that implies.
A symphony of love and life
    Was dancing in her eyes.
I lost my heart but not my head;
    I bid her fond adieu
For she was only twenty-three
    While I was sixty-two.

A Symphony of Love and Life

She was sweet and twenty-three with all that that implies,—

was dancing in her eyes.

—Excerpt: OUT OF SEASON
Wm Spicer

79

DO YOU recall when first we met,
THE So many years ago?
FIRST OF We promised then we'd not forget...
But THEN how could we know?
Everything, I loved the grass whereon you walked
I loved the air you breathed
I heard music when you talked,
Your face was love-enwreathed.
The magic of your being near!
The eyes where love was spelt
Were lake-like mirrors crystal clear,
Where secretly I knelt.

Do you recall when first we met?
No thought of sad goodbye,
No thought of hurting or regret
No thought of parting's "why?".
Through all the many years of change,
Time will never thieve
The loving moments, nor will stop
Their tugging at my sleeve,
For like a lovely dream that's dreamed,
Then flees before the dawn,
They go to come like love redeemed;
What wretch would say, "They're GONE?".

Do you recall when first we met?
The first of Fall or Spring?
The first of June? I won't forget...
The first of everything.

You

I strolled through a garden of roses,
 Roses of every known hue.
I studied each, pensive; would it be offensive
 To say that I saw only you?

I walked through the trees and the forest;
 Fresh with the pine-scented air.
I stood all amazed at the scene as I gazed,
 For you were all that was there.

Undaunted, I turned to the masters
 With thoughts of rhetorical grace;
The lines became blurred until never a word
 Was there but reflected your face.

I sought through the secret of silence
 A respite from life's weary trial.
In the quiet of thought Omnipotence wrought;
 Like magic, a wonder... your smile.

⸙ LOVE'S DEFINITION ⸙

Beauty could be cotton clouds
    Above a sea of green,
Or rolling foothills topped with pines,
    With fields of grain between;
It could be crescent moon romancing
    With the Evening Star—
I'd find the magic of your smile
    More beautiful by far.

Loneliness might be a dove,
    Or dog without a boy;
It might be Adam without Eve,
    Or Helen without Troy.
It might seem red and white be lonely
    With no field of blue,
But most of all would I be lonely
    If there were no you.

❧ IF I HAD MY WAY ❧

I would live to be a hundred.

I would see the sunset flare,
Note the changes of the seasons
        And the silver in your hair.

I would feel the cool of evening
And the warmth of summer wine.
I would know the loving comfort
        Of your gentle hand in mine.

I would smell the breath of roses,
Hear the sassy jay complain
Taste the sweetness of the honey
        And your kisses once again.

I would live to be a hundred,
Keep my senses sharp and true
That I might know the years of sharing
        Every joy of life with you.

Anniversary Thought

I'm grateful for the sweetest years
    That I have ever known!
Like perfume in a summer breeze,
    So swiftly have they flown!
Tender moments, touch of hand
    Kindness, gentle mien,
Hours of sharing loving thoughts,
    Happy, safe, serene!

Little thought of years behind
    With bleak and barren care;
Eyes and hearts and hands ahead
    Love-life everywhere!
Today I see from where I stand
    A world I've never known!
Except in dreams. And what a world
    Of fragrance, grace and tone!

Thanks for all the things you are
    And what I'm bound to be
Because of you, because of love,
    Because you came to me →!

for all the
things you are,
and what
I'm bound
to be

THANKS

because of you

"ANNIVERSARY
THOUGHTS"
WM. SPICER

because of love
because you came to me!

A Song of PARTING

We've sung our song together, Darling,
    Shared the selfsame stage,
And made such lovely harmony —
    It's hard to turn the page.

Our love song had it's tender tones,
    A dissonant or two;
I sometimes phrased a little soon
    Or maybe missed a cue.

But whether it were happy note
    Or bit of solemn verse,
You always did quite naturally
    What others must rehearse.

If there need be a closing cadence
    To the song we sing,
Well, let it be a joyful sound,
    Like church bells in the spring.

And when the notes have gently fallen
    Like a summer rain,
Refreshing every memory,
    Perhaps we'll sing again

BETRAYED

I wore my heart
  Upon my sleeve
in view where all could see
    I never
tried to hide my thoughts
from those who trusted me
    BUT TRUST
is not a one-way street
  I learned the lesson well
    MY THOUGHTS
And trust were both betrayed
My heart was dragged through hell.

TO A LOST LOVE

Dull duty holds my hand today
    And bids me love and live.
But what I gave so freely once
    Is now not mine to give.
Though other hearts and others' lives
    Become a part of mine,
There cannot be a heart or life
    To take the place of thine.

I walk again in memory
    The paths we knew so well
And how I loved thy gentle touch
    These lips can never tell.
And now, as then, the tender tears
    Unbidden freely flow,
A witness of the love we shared
    So very long ago.

Between us two the chasm fixed
    Defies our sacred vow
And what we cherished then the fates
    Will never more allow,
But could I make that pledge again,
    May heaven witness be,
I'd take thee as I took thee then
    For all eternity.

BUT COULD I MAKE THAT PLEDGE AGAIN

May heaven witness be, I'd take thee As I took thee Then For all Eternity

Excerpt: TO A LOST LOVE
WM. SPICER

89

FOLIO FIVE

BELIEVING
& Fulfillment

The Enrichment of

BELIEVING &

The Fulfillment

FOLIO FIVE

BELIEVING

JUST IN CASE

"There is No GOD,"
I heard him say,
IT'S ALL a pack of lies,
And those who think there is a GOD
will get a BIG SURPRISE",

"I don't have all the answers yet,
But just BETWEEN US TWO,
I'd rather think he's wrong,
IN CASE
there is one, wouldn't you?"

HOPE
LOVE
LIFE
ETERNAL

Two Men

He was a favored of men,
    GAUNT AND STRONG AND FEARLESS.
He spoke with a sword.
    EMPIRES WERE FORGED, KINGDOMS WERE SHAKEN.
He was revered and respected.
    WHEN DEATH CAME, IT CAME WITH HONOR.

What was his name?
EVEN THE GODS HAVE FORGOTTEN

He was a favored of God,
    COMELY, KIND AND GENTLE.
He spoke of truth and life
    AND A HEAVENLY KINGDOM.
He was despised and rejected.
    DEATH WAS CRUEL, SLOW AND SHAMEFUL.

What was his name?
IT IS HOPE, LOVE AND LIFE ETERNAL

The Search

"God is a fancy," the fool sighed.

He went to the city that man had made
Of mortar, steel and glass.
He labored and suffered and knew his kind.
The shop was his temple and gold his god.
His heart was old before his time;
His life was baren and dry.

"This is real and all," he cried,
And turning his face to the wall, he died.

96

"There must be a God," the wise man said.

He went to the hills that God had made.
He drank of the fresh-water stream
And he breathed the air
Of the fir and pine.
The tented sky was his temple.
His heart was light and his life a joy.

He looked at the beauty before him spread
"This is the house of God", he said.

I know...

...there is a torch that I can light.
I know there is a wrong that I can right.
I know a loving thought that I can share.

ARE THESE NOT BURDENS
I AM BOUND TO BEAR?

Excerpt: THE PRISONER
Wm. Spicer

98

The Prisoner

I know the truth but has it set me free?
  Am I not bound by what I know to be?
  Have I not fashioned me an albatross
  In knowing Jesus suffered on the cross?

I know there is a torch that I can light.
  I know there is a wrong that I can right.
  I know a loving thought that I can share.
  Are these not burdens I am bound to bear?

I watch the fingers of the sun at play
  Upon a harp of clouds at close of day.
  Come, tell me of the blind who cannot see
  A setting sun, then tell me I am free.

Although by gifts of freedom I be crowned,

  Through Him who came to free me
                              I am bound.

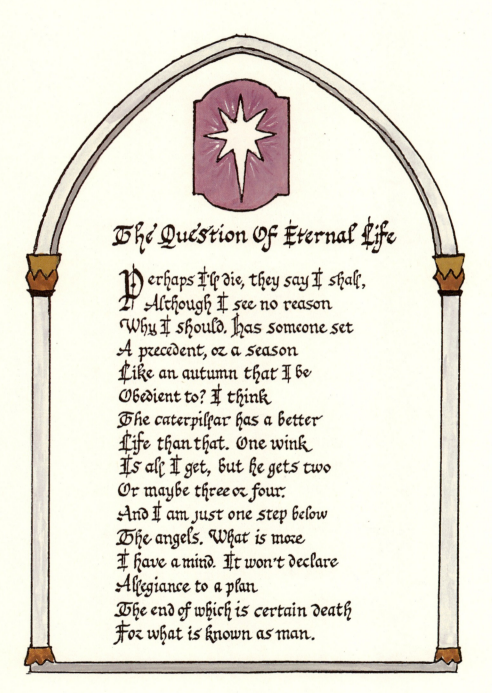

The Question Of Eternal Life

Perhaps I'll die, they say I shall,
Although I see no reason
Why I should. Has someone set
A precedent, or a season
Like an autumn that I be
Obedient to? I think
The caterpillar has a better
Life than that. One wink
Is all I get, but he gets two
Or maybe three or four.
And I am just one step below
The angels. What is more
I have a mind. It won't declare
Allegiance to a plan
The end of which is certain death
For what is known as man.

I've given thought to what is called
"Eternal life", that they
Who press the cause of such a state
Are also first to say
That I must die. And so I ponder:
Did the Master die
That he might live again, or did
he suffer death that I
Might have a life eternal? Where,
In all this sacred word,
Did he say I must die?

                      I grant
A voice is seldom heard
To echo what was uttered there
Of life's eternal spring,
But I for one can hear it now:
"O death, where is thy sting?"

THE SPIRAL CIRCLE

"What's the hurry, Bill?" she asked.
  "You cannot learn it all.
The seed that sprouts in early spring
    Is seedling still when fall
And winter take their toll. The snow
    Banks hide it from the sun
For one full season. Is it dead?
    Its life has just begun.

"And what are you that you should know
    The secret will of God?
He placed you here with toddling feet.
    You're still too young to plod
The path His Son was wont to walk.
    Your brief three-score-and-ten
Is just a step. It is not yours
    To know the why and when.

"The pine where eagles nest and breed
Was first the Word and then a seed."

IS each each hour spent a Mockery?
Do I seek in vain?
vain vain? in vain?

Excerpt: MY SECRET PATH
wms. Spicer

103

My Secret Path

I have waited long and patient
    For a certain sign.
I have sought the varied byways
    For the life named MINE.

I have plumbed the deepest gorges,
    Followed nameless creeks,
Blazed a trail where none has ventured,
    Scaled the highest peaks.

I have studied every pathway
    With the greatest care
In the hope that what I'm seeking
    May be hidden there.

Is each hour spent a mockery?
    Do I seek in vain?
Did it call while I was sleeping?
    Will it call again?

Will it find me anxious, waiting?
    Will my heart rejoice?
Or will I, through negligence,
    Never hear the voice?

I walked today in fertile field,
    Where flowers bloom and blow
And make their little part of world
    A verdant cameo.
I found a quiet, lonely place,
    And there, with brooding heart,
I found the essence of my life,
    I found my counterpart.

I felt my inmost soul, my spirit,
    Haltingly entreat:
"What does this soul have to give
    To make a life complete?"
No sooner had the question formed
    Than answer took its place
And drift'd into my consciousness,
    And left without a trace...
"Be a friend, a different kind,
    Wedded to the soul;
Let your heart be love-enshrined
    Beatitude the goal;
Make your life a garden for
    The temple; then consign
All, a sacred, living flame,
    To burn within the shrine."

I walked today in fertile field,
    Where flowers bloom and blow.
I had a talk with God today,
    And now I know...I know.

I walked today in fertile field,
Where flowers bloom and blow,
I had a talk with God today
and now I know I know . . .

—Excerpt: THE ANSWER
Wm. Spicer

106

FULFILLMENT

THE NEW SONG

MY EYES WERE CLOSED, YET I COULD SEE
BEYOND THE WALLS THAT BOUNDED ME,
BEYOND THE FIELDS AND HILLS THAT MADE
MY WORLD, BEYOND THE SKIES THAT FADE
INTO ETERNITY.

      I SAW
A HAND REACH OUT AND GENTLY DRAW
THE HEAVENS BACK REVEALING THERE
MY PAST LIFE LIVED, THE WHEN AND WHERE
OF EVERY MOMENT. EVERY THOUGHT
AND EVERY WISH AND WORD WERE CAUGHT
AND HELD WHERE I COULD SEE AND HEAR
A PAGEANT OF MY PAST: THERE FEAR
AND DOUBT WERE SIDE BY SIDE WITH HOPE;
INSPIRED THOUGHT WAS MADE TO GROPE
THE PATH OF CARELESS ACTION; HATE
AND LOVE WALKED HAND IN HAND; WHILE FATE
AND RESOLUTION PLAYED THEIR GAME,
MY LIFE, THEIR PAWN, LIVED ON THE SAME.

MY EYES WERE CLOSED, YET I COULD SEE
BEYOND THE WORLD THAT BOUNDED ME.
I SAW EACH CONSCIOUS THOUGHT AND WORD
BECAME REALITY. I HEARD
AND UNDERSTOOD THE SONG THAT I
MUST WRITE AND SING. NOT BY-AND-BY
BUT NOW.

          MY GOD IS TRUTH. I KNOW
I WORSHIP THAT. AND IT IS SO.

MY GOD IS TRUTH . . .

Excerpt: THE NEW SONG
WM SPICER

109

~ LOVE ~

Love will not tolerate tolerance
Or suffer a vows "give or take"
Love is not wrought,
stolen or bought.
Love will not founder or quake.
Love is not balanced or measured,
having no standards or rules.
Love can be taken,
rejected, forsaken
Possessed by both sages and fools.

Love is a smile of disinterest,
Respecter of nothing and none.
Love can be learned,
love can be earned,
But cannot be wagered and won.
Love is a fountain artesian,
it needs neither query nor nod
It bears without reason,
nurture or season.
Love is the offspring of God.

Love is the offspring of God

Excerpt: LOVE
Wm. SPICER

OH GOD,
might I for one brief moment know
The MYSTIC PEACE that Jesus came to share;
The life He gave that mortal could not take;
The PROMISE that through
Him I can be heir
To Life ETERNAL; and the sacrifice
He suffered when they nailed him to the tree;
HIS GENTLENESS,
compassion, love sublime;
AND WHAT I AM that He would die for me.

THE SUPPLIANT PRAYS

112

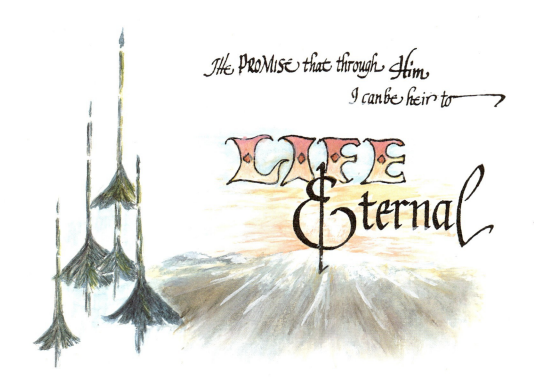

The PROMISE that through Him
I can be heir to ⟶

LIFE
Eternal

And what I am that He would die for me.
Excerpt: The Suppliant Prays
Wm Spicer

Part III

THE TIDES OF CHALLENGE

118

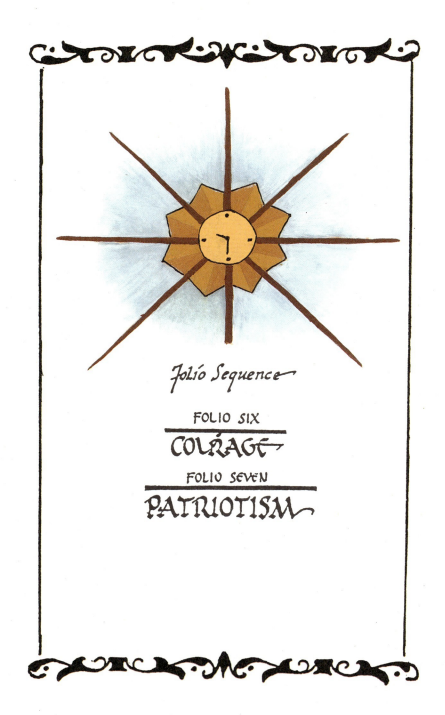

Folio Sequence

FOLIO SIX
COURAGE

FOLIO SEVEN
PATRIOTISM

FOLIO SIX

COURAGE

The Inspiration of
COURAGE &
Commitment to *Striving*

FOLIO SIX

COURAGE

TO THOSE WHO LOSE
    QUOTE
THE LOW-DOWN TRUTH
SOLITUDE
    QUOTE
THE "MIGHT HAVE BEEN"
THE NUMBER ONE PRO

TO THOSE WHO LOSE

It's no disgrace to lose the race
   if you will give your best.
if you can smile when every mile
   is torture, that's the test.
if you can give until you're spent
   and never count the cost,
You may not cross the finish line
   but, friend, you haven't lost.

it isn't shame to lose the game,
   no matter what the score,
if you can take what's handed out
   and come right back for more.
you hit the mud
   and taste the blood,
you bet, I'll buy the dinner,
   you may not place or even show
   but, friend, you'll be a winner.

YOU
NEVER REALLY
POSSESS a
DESIRE
Until...
the
desire possesses you!

THE LOW-DOWN TRUTH

It's not important what you see
    But rather how you see it.
You saw a fight? That's well and good,
    But did you referee it?
You may have had a ring-side seat,
    And looked with all your might;
But what you saw from where you sat
    Was only half a fight.

Get in the ring, that's where it is,
    If you can stand the gaff,
And feel the sweat and taste the blood;
    Now that's the other half.
You ask the man who sees the fight;
    Opinions by the minute.
But if you want the low-down truth,
    You ask the man who's in it.

SOLITUDE

The seeker sings in loneliness:
　Not sad or plaintive wails
But the clear, clean tones of a hungry heart,
　Like the changing wind in the sails
Of an eager yawl, now high on the crest
　Of hope, now low and dead
In a doldrum of pitiless quest.

　　　　　　　　　　　　Sing on,
　Sing on, but do not dread
The loneliness. The social mold
　Is made for lesser souls.
They sing the Song Of Life alone
　Who claim the highest goals.

Life
—like nature—
reserves
ITS' MASTERPIECES
FOR THOSE WHO LEAVE
THE TRAIL

THE "MIGHT HAVE BEEN"

The "might have been" look back at life
When the race is all but run
And feel regret for having left
So many things undone.
They worry about "three score and ten"
And plan each hour they give it,
But when the allotted time expires
They haven't begun to live it.

128

They hesitate at something new
    Because there is no rule.
They won't improve what has been done
    Because of ridicule.
They falter when it's time to plant
    For fear there be a drought. . .
Was ever there a ship came in
    That was not first sent out?

The moral of my story is:
    Don't mind who ballyhoo it,
If you've a job you wish to do,
    Why, go ahead and do it.
For what is life but what we do
    And how and where and when?
There'll never be a monument
    To one who "might have been".

~ don't mind
who ballyhoo it
if you've a Job
you wish to do..
why
go ahead
and
do it !

Excerpt: THE "MIGHT HAVE BEEN"
WM. SPICER

THE NUMBER ONE PRO

Everyone knows you for what you can do,
    But nobody knows what you are.
They see the routine of a well-tuned machine,
    They shout and hurrah every show, every scene,
But they never see all the work in between;
    And that is the best show by far.

Everyone's looking but they never see,
    They listen but they never hear.
What audience shares in the heartaches and prayers?
    And who feels the failure that purges and tears?
Nobody feels it and nobody cares;
    They come just to watch you — and cheer.

The mountain is yours, you have challenged and won.
    And it was a hell of a show.
You started a "bit" and ended a "hit",
    A measure of luck and a whole lot of grit;
Your motto was 'win it', and you wouldn't quit.
    That makes you a number one pro.

FOLIO SEVEN

PATRIOTISM

THE PRIDE OF
PATRIOTISM &
DEDICATION TO *Freedom & Peace*

FOLIO SEVEN

PATRIOTISM

QUOTE: Patrick Henry
A VOICE FOR THE AGES
THE STATUE
    OF LIBERTY SPEAKS

"Sign Not only for yourselves, BUT FOR ALL AGES for that parchment will be the textbook of freedom — the Bible for the rights of men forever?"

PATRICK HENRY
·JULY 4, 1776·

135

A Voice For The Ages

HEN IN THE COURSE OF HUMAN STRIFE

A PEOPLE FIND ITS PLACE
    AND FEEL THE "ONENESS WITH ITS KIND"
THAT COMES WITH FREEDOM'S GRACE,

LET ARMIES MARCH AND MONARCHS FLAUNT
    PROFANE OR SACRED LAWS,
THERE IS NO FORCE TO STAY A TIDE
    THAT SWELLS WITH SUCH A CAUSE.

THE DAM OF GREED AND PRIDE WAS HIGH,
    AND THE WATERS OF FREEDOM CHOKED
IN THEIR NATURAL FLOW. IN ROYAL DISGUISE
    THE EVIL OF MAN WAS CLOAKED.

NO LONGER THE ECHOED SONG OF THE FIELD,
    NO LONGER THE HEARTH'S APPEAL
WHERE FAMILY GATHERED TO LAUGH AND PRAY,
    FOR THEIRS WAS THE TYRANT'S HEEL.

BUT THIS WAS A RARE AND BLOODED BREED
    WITH VALOR AND GREATNESS TO SPARE,
AND A NEW FLAME BURNED IN THE HEART OF EACH,
AND A NEW SONG FILLED THE AIR.

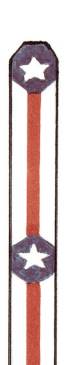

THESE GENTLEMEN, BY HARDSHIP TEMPERED,
        WOULD NOT BEND THE KNEE
TO DESPOT KING OR PRINCE OR LORD,
        BUT CRIED OUT, "WE ARE FREE!"

"WHENCE CAME YOUR SO-CALLED 'SACRED RIGHTS'
        THAT THROUGH A BIRTHRIGHT, GAVE
TO ONE THE NAME OF 'NOBLEMAN'
        AND TO ANOTHER 'SLAVE'?

"WHETHER IN EMBELLISHED HALL
        OR STANDING HOE IN HAND,
NOBLE MEN ARE NOBLE STILL
        NO MATTER WHERE THEY STAND.

"PERHAPS THE SUN has NEVER SET
        ON YOUR ILL-GOTTEN MIGHT,
BUT NATURE DOES NOT SMILE ON HIM
        WHO LIVE THE PARASITE,

"SO MUSTER WHAT YOU WILL. WE'LL FIGHT
        WITH WHAT AND WHERE YOU PLEASE,
FOR WE WOULD SOONER SUFFER DEATH
        THAN LIVE UPON OUR KNEES."

WAS EVER THERE SO GREAT A CALL,
        SO FIERCE A DECLARATION?
THE WORDS HAVE ECHOED ROUND THE WORLD
        TO EVERY CLIME AND NATION.

NO MASSIVE MARBLE MONUMENT,
        NO GRAND APOSTROPHE
CAN MARK THEIR PLACE. THEIR VERY DUST
        IS CALLING, "WE ARE FREE!"

137

WE ARE Free!

WE THE PEOPLE...

The Statue of Liberty Speaks

"AMERICA, I'VE WATCHED YOUR DOINGS
NEARLY FROM YOUR BIRTH.
I'VE SEEN YOUR FORTUNE GIVING HOPE
TO EVERY SOUL ON EARTH.

I'VE SEEN YOU TAKE THE HOMELESS IN,
I'VE SEEN YOU FIRST TO GIVE.
BUT DO YOU HAVE A RIGHT TO ORDER
HOW THE REST SHALL LIVE?

THERE'S CHAOS IN SOUTH-AFRICA;
    ITS PROBLEMS YOU BEMOAN.
YOUR CONGRESS MEETS TO SOLVE THE PLIGHT,
    BUT WHAT ABOUT YOUR OWN?

THE NEAR EAST IS A WRITHING MASS.
    WHAT GOOD TO INTERVENE?
YOU FLEX YOUR MUSCLE, CALL FOR PEACE
    WHERE PEACE HAS NEVER BEEN.

YOU ACT THE PART OF BUSYBODY.
    WHO GAVE YOU THE RIGHT
TO SIT IN JUDGMENT OVER NATIONS
    THAT ELECT TO FIGHT?

"THE SHOT HEARD 'ROUND THE WORLD" WAS YOURS,
    THE FIGHTING AT THE SOMME,
YOURS "THE BATTLE OF THE BULGE",
    AND FINALLY "THE BOMB".

COUNT THE WARS THAT YOU HAVE FOUGHT.
    WHICH NATIONS COUNSELED YOU?
THEY'D EASIER CHANGE THE COLORS OF
    YOUR CRIMSON, WHITE AND BLUE.

SO TRIM MY LAMP AND GIVE ME OIL
    AND LET OLD GLORY FLY;
RESPECT ALL NATIONS, TEND YOUR OWN,
    AND "KEEP YOUR POWDER DRY."

INTERMISSION

The Lights Are Dimmed
It's Curtain Time

Part IV

MOODS OF REFLECTION

MOODS
OF
REFLECTION

FOLIOS
VIII · IX · X

Folio Sequence

FOLIO EIGHT

SORROW
& Fate

FOLIO NINE

MEMORIES

FOLIO TEN

LIVE

FOLIO EIGHT

SORROW & Fate

The Melancholy of

SORROW &

The Hand of Fate

FOLIO EIGHT

SORROW

LINCOLN'S LOST LOVE
OF TREES AND MEN
THE AGNOSTIC

THE STING
-THE HAND OF FATE-

LIVE
THE GAMBLER
THE NIGHTSONG
OF A WANDERER
MY DESIRE
WHEN I HAVE GONE

LINCOLN'S LOST LOVE

The school-house bell is quiet now,
The farmer, hat in hand,
Has left the field. The cattle all
        Like living statues stand,
        The village bows its head.
No more miller's happy greeting;
Gone the thrush's note,
The song that echoed through the meadow
        Silent in its throat,
        In homage to the dead.

The icy hands of death have closed
The eyes of gentle Ann.
The spring of wedding promise spreads
        Its blossoms where she ran
        And where she lies asleep.
There was no fear of him who takes,
Or plea to powers that give;
Just one last sigh for her who loved
        So very much to live
        And left so much to reap.

A simple marker shows her place
Among the Rutledge weeds.
And the time has shown no mercy. Nothing
        Grows where memory feeds;
        Nirvana is the god.
But when the springtime spread its blossoms
On the meadow green,
A lonely Lincoln dreamed about
        The wife who might have been,
        Who slept beneath the sod.

OF TREES AND MEN

His summer season's done. And all
   The beauties of a welcome fall
Unfold before his tired eyes.

The oaks against the billowed skies
Seem pleased, and wear their final best
Of gold and brown. The maple, dressed
In red, ignores the yearly threat
And dances on. There's no regret
Who trust there'll still be other springs.

His summer season's done. He sings
No final anthem. But the charms
Of fall he greets with open arms.

THE AGNOSTIC

She sits among her memories and waits.

How like the last of summer's gifts, the rose.
Its tender petals falling one by one
To final rest beneath the winter snows:
How like the closing hours, the dusk of day,
When evening hangs its curtain in the sky.
And who can call back one sweet moment now,
Or plumb the ages of a by-and-by,
Or prove that she will live again and see
The loved ones who are gone? She'll say, "The Fates
Will care for that, I only hope."

                              And so
She sits among her memories and waits.

The Sting

It could be winter on a southern key
    Or summer on a northern stretch or strait
    That he who visits all will call on me.
    Will I be ready be it soon or late?

There'll be no prior notice, word or sign
    That I might get accounts all squared away
    There'll be no time for final tear or wine;
    I'll never know the hour or the day.

They say he comes when he's the least expected,
    Like a twister on a Kansas plain,
    And that his suit has never been rejected;
    Never has he heard, "Please call again."

    I wonder, would we fear that final door
    If we had finished all we came here for?

the Hand of Fate

LIVE

Laugh and love and sing and sigh;
Cherish living till you die.
Don't go courting want and care,
There is plenty and to spare
Let him tend to troubles who
Can't find better things to do.

Don't be "life's proportion's" slave
Losing what you wish to save;
Time has ways of making known
Just how many years have flown.
Question not that moments fly,
Cherish living till you die.

THE GAMBLER

I'd like to think that when my time
        As citizen of Earth
Expires I shall have done a job
        That bears the mark of worth;
No monumental work defying
        Time, but something done
That shows my stay a little more
        Than just a race well run.

What could I feel except regret
        If all my years were spent
Providing keep? The birds do that.
        There'll be another rent
Come due, and I shall give account
        Of gifts left unrefined,
Of time misused, of thoughtless word
        And gods that I've enshrined

I'd like to feel I'd paid my dues,
        Had come out free and clear,
And shown a little profit for
        The time I've spent down here.
But should my tally come up short,
        I'll blame the circumstance,
And trust that god is fair enough
        To give me one more chance.

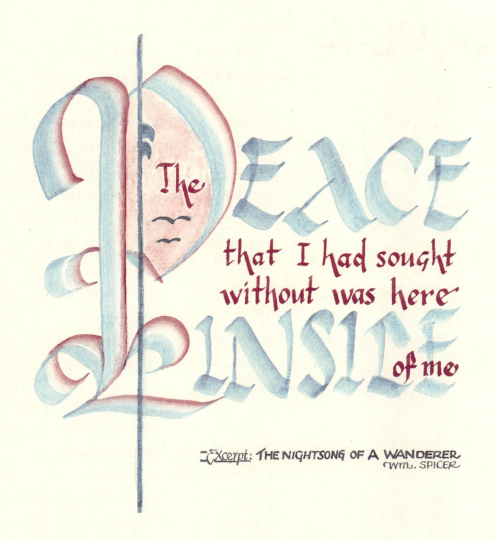

The Peace that I had sought without was here inside of me

Excerpt: THE NIGHTSONG OF A WANDERER
WM. SPICER

160

THE NIGHTSONG OF A WANDERER

When I was young my heart was free;
   I never had a care.
I sought the beauty of the world
   And found it everywhere.
But now the freedom that I knew,
   The voice that bade me roam,
Is silent and my weary eyes
   Have turned to scenes of home.

When I was young I thought that peace
   Was something one must earn—
A yield or harvest to be gathered
   As a life's return.
But now I see with older eyes
   What youth could never see—
The peace that I had sought without
   Was here inside of me.

My DESIRE

I've a passion to stand by a mountain falls
Where the waters dash and spring
Like a freightened deer, where the eagle soars
And the ponderosa cling
To the sky.

I've a longing to breathe an air
That's refreshing, cool and clean,
Where the only perfume is the pine tree pitch
Or the spicy wintergreen
Or the dogwood profuse with its scented stars
Or the rich magnolia bloom.

My desire is to spend what is left of life
Where there's time to think and room
For a body to stretch. I have paid my way,
I have worked out duty's task.
I would spend what is left in the hills of God.
And is that too much to ask?

I would spend what is left in the hills of God

Is that too much to ask?

EXCERPT: MY DESIRE
Wm Spicer

163

WHEN I HAVE GONE

Don't weep when I have gone.
                          These bones
Are hardly worth a tear.
A few years hence and who will know
Or care that I was here
And struggled through my share of life.
For what is this you see
But some old garment soiled and worn?
I trust the real me is made of better stuff.
                          Perhaps
There'll be a secret spot
In some far recess of your soul,
A sort of Camelot,
Where all your finest memories dwell;
And there the only part
That's worth a tear will find a place
To live on in your heart.

Remember this, and do not mourn
The change, there is a dawn
That follows every setting sun.

Don't weep when I have gone.

THERE IS A DAWN
that follows every
SETTING
SUN.

dont weep when I have gone

Excerpt: WHEN I HAVE GONE
WM. SPICER

165

MEMORIES

The Nostalgia of
MEMORIES
& The Pain of Progress

FOLIO NINE

MEMORIES

COLORS OF MAY
GOLDEN MEMORIES
BOOK OF DREAMS

I DIED A LITTLE BIT TODAY

— THE PAIN OF PROGRESS —

WHEN I WAS JES' A KID
HIDDEN TREASURE
MORE TO BE DONE
HAD I A CHOICE
BROTHERS
EVERGREEN CORNER
A CHRISTMAS DREAM

Excerpt: Golden Memories
Wm. Spicer

High-tension cables sweep the skies
WHERE EAGLE ONCE WAS King

Colors of May

The Years
　　　have a way of just stealing
along like the closing of day
　　　or the fading
　　away of the seasons.
　　　　　But fade ————————
as they will, there's a song
in my heart that is
　　　stronger than steel.

　　　　　　Like the ray
of the sun reaching back
　　for a final display
on a blanket of clouds
　　whether swaddling or shroud
my reflections of thought
　　are the colors of may.
　　　and the colors of may

170

are the shouting
aloud to the
pastures of green,
and the fields freshly plowed;
and the meadowlark
singing, the chapel bells
ringing
their message of praise
down the valley endowed
with the beauty
of spring

though the
years will be bringing
their summons of age,
I will look to the
stinging of death as the
start, and
the future just part
of the past
and the colors of may
will be clinging like
yesterday's love
to the song in my heart

GOLDEN MEMORIES

High-tension cables sweep the skies
WHERE EAGLE ONCE WAS KING.
The songbirds leave the meadows, once
THEIR HOME, AND SADLY SING
A last good-bye. What was is now
BUT WALLS OF GLASS AND STONE,
Cement and iron, cold and dead.

What building can atone
FOR ALL THE BEAUTY LOST: THE PATH
That went down to the creek,
THE HILL BEHIND WHERE CATTLE GRAZED,
The distant mountain peak
WE TOOK FOR GRANTED, SALMONBERRY
Patches?

172

These are gone.
THE PATH IS NOW A BLACKTOP STREET.
A manufactured lawn
IS WHERE THE CATTLE FED. THE STREAM
That ran so sparkling clear
IS NOW AN ALLEY STREWN WITH TRASH
And garbage. You will hear
NO SONGBIRD SING; THE TRAFFIC RACKET
Grates and grinds.

I'm glad
I LIVED BEFORE THIS THING CALLED PROGRESS
Took its toll. I had
IT ALL. I HAVE IT STILL; THE HUNGRY
Senses of my youth
LEFT NOTHING UNPERCEIVED, AND GARNERED
Nature's slightest truth,
AND BOUND IT FAST, I KNOW NOT HOW,
With memory's golden chain,
THAT I MIGHT SEE AND HEAR
And LIVE it all again

BOOK OF DREAMS

MOVE ON YOU SAY? I have moved on,
    For I'm three times your age.
I just stopped by to reminisce
    And add another page
To memory's book of dreams.

                How like
    A medley of old-time lays
The scenes return to feed my soul
    The bread of better days.
No cattle graze where yesterday
    The pasture-land was green;
No wily hawk his hunting plies.
    How long since there has been
A haystack or a drying shock
    Where once the cornfield lay?

I think this is the very spot
      Where I would come to play
When just a child. Across the meadow
      I can see the church,
Its glistening white against the green,
      And there the patch of birch
Close by the well, the woodpile handy
      By the kitchen door;
And there's the buggy where we left it
      'Neath the sycamore.

But now I close my book of dreams;
      The life that was is gone,
My soul is fed.

                  Move on, you say?
      Ah yes, I must move on.

I DIED A LITTLE BIT TODAY

A LITTLE OF ME DIED TODAY—

    The park where children romp and play,
    From youngster down to toddling tot,
    Will be a public parking lot.
    It seems our town has felt the weight
    Of growth. I cannot help but hate
    The creeping plague where malls and marts
    Infect and claim the choicest parts,
    The parts that nature set aside.
    But trees and grass and swings and slide
    Must go. The business banner flies.
    And so, a little of me dies.

We form committees, plead our case:
    Do growing children have no place?
    Must they spend all their time inside
    Walled homes? The city could provide.
    The children need the trees and skies
    And space to race and exercise.
The council renders its decision:
    Kids can watch the television.

Do you wonder why I say,
    I died a little bit today?

THE PAIN OF PROGRESS —

WHEN
I
WAS
JES'
A
KID

Things ain't like they used t' be
When I was jes a kid.
Why shucks, I'd take my fishin'-pole
From where I had it hid
N head off down t' where the branch
Went cuttin' 'cross the place,
'N' me 'n' Shep would find a spot
T' fish, 'n' not a trace.
O' nothin' 'ceptin' worms 'n' shade
N log t' lean agin';
The whole thing jes fer kids like me.
You bet, that's where I bin.

I caint he'p thinkin' how the things
What was jes ain't no more.
'N' kids today, in my opinion,
Grows up mighty poor.
The TV ain't no substeetute
Fer hikin' down the creek,
'R climbin' 'long the ol' stump-fence,
'R playin' hide-'n'-seek.

I often wonder how it happened,
That the folks got rid
O' all the things we used t' do
When I was jes' a kid.

178

I often wonder how it happened,
That the folks got rid
O' all the things we used t' do
When I was jes' a kid.

Excerpt: WHEN I WAS JES' A KID
Wm. Spicer

179

HIDDEN TREASURE

What has become of the beauty I knew:
   The trees and the shrubs
         and the flowers that grew
All along every roadway,
      so uninterrupted
For mile after mile,
       through the fields uncorrupted
Where song-birds nested
      and nurtured their young,
Where the Black Angus grazed,
      and the wild-roses clung
To the post and the rail,
      where the air smelled as clean
As the corn freshly husked
      or the ripe wintergreen?
And where are the pleasures
      of farmhouse and shed:
With a turn at the churn
      and the taste of the bread
While still hot from the oven,
      the bed in the loft

Where the covers were spread
  on the hay, and as soft
As the moonlight that filtered
  through the cracks in the walls
Of the barn, and the milk-house,
  the corn-crib and stalls?
Yes, where are the neighbors
  that I knew so well:
Like the pastor who couldn't
  help stopping to tell
Us the story of God and His love,
  and the people
Who gathered each Wednesday to pray
  'neath the steeple
That served as a landmark?
      Oh Time in your flight
Tell me, what have you done
  with those years of delight?
Is my memory the answer?
      shall I never find
All those treasures again
      except in my mind?

MORE TO BE DONE

Eyes that scarce could see the sun
As it sank in the evening sky;
Shoulders that showed the weight of years;
Hands all withered and dry;
Hair as white as snow on the hill;
Cheeks like those of the dead;
The old man managed a dry little smile,
And these are the words he said:

"IDLE AND WAITING AND WALKING THE DOG!
  THIS ISN'T THE LIFE FOR ME.
I GUESS, BY RIGHTS, WITH LIFE MOST GONE,
  IT'S ABOUT WHERE I SHOULD BE;
BUT SOMETHING KEEPS WHISPERING DEEP DOWN INSIDE
  AND TELLS ME THERE'S MORE TO BE DONE.
AND REALLY, WITH HONESTY, WHAT CAN I SHOW
  THAT'S ANYTHING MORE THAN BEGUN?
A LIFETIME OF LABOR, ANOTHER OF LOVE,
  AN OUTLINE OF SOMETHING I DREAMED,
A POEM, A PICTURE, A THOUGHT THAT WAS NEW,
  ANOTHER NOT HALF WHAT IT SEEMED,
A MOMENT OF PLEASURE, ANOTHER OF PAIN,
  WITH HEARTACHES AND BACKACHES, — AND THEN
A SUNSET THAT LOOKS LIKE A SUNRISE TO ME,
  AND I'M READY TO START OUT AGAIN.

"WHERE AM I GOING? WHY THE CONCERN?
  HAVEN'T I LIVED MY SHARE?
WHAT'S WRONG WITH WAITING AND WALKING THE DOG,
  OR JUST LEANING BACK IN MY CHAIR

AND DREAMING OF JOYS OF BY-GONE DAYS,
  AND THINKING OF PLACES I'VE BEEN,
AND FACES OF FRIENDS THAT I ALL BUT FORGOT,
  AND PICTURING PASTURES SERENE;
THE TRAILING ARBUTUS AND OLD STUMP FENCE,
  AND LILAC DOWN CLOSE TO THE WELL,

183

THE SANDHILL CRANE LIKE A SHIP IN THE SKY,
    AND THE BUTTERNUT THERE WHERE IT FELL,
THE CELLAR WHERE MA ALWAYS KEPT THE PRESERVES,
    THE MILK-HOUSE WITH CROCKS FULL OF CREAM,
THE SMOKE-HOUSE, A SAFE WAY BACK FROM THE BARN,
    WITH HAMS HANGING DOWN FROM THE BEAM?

"OF COURSE I KNOW THERE'S NOT MUCH LEFT
    OF THE THINGS THAT USED TO BE;
THE SAND-HILL CRANE AND THE OLD STUMP FENCE
    ARE ONLY A MEMORY.
I KNOW THAT THE HOUSE IS LONG SINCE GONE;
    THE CELLAR IS ONLY A HOLE;
A WALL IS ALL THAT REMAINS OF THE BARN—
    THE YEARS HAVE TAKEN THEIR TOLL.
THE YEARS HAVE TAKEN THEIR TOLL OF MORE
    THAN THE PLACE WHERE I USED TO DWELL;
THE VOICES ARE SILENT, THE FACES ARE GONE
    OF THOSE I LOVED SO WELL.
SHE, AS THE LILAC, WITHERED AND DIED,
    HER VOICE HAS LONG BEEN STILL
WHOSE LOVE I KNEW. MY HEART IS THERE,
    BURIED WITH HER ON THE HILL."

HE GENTLY TUGGED AT THE LEASH IN HIS HAND
    AS HE LOOKED AT THE DYING SUN;
THE OLD MAN MANAGED A DRY LITTLE SMILE
    "COME, SHEP, THERE'S MORE TO BE DONE."

HAD I A CHOICE

I'D RATHER THINGS BE AS THEY WERE
    When I was in my youth.
How cleanly separated then
    Were fantasy and truth.

I knew the trees that graced the hill
    But not as oak and pine,
And more than concord were the grapes
    That hung beneath the vine.

No weatherman to prophesy
    A vagrant hurricane.
But Father's corns were gospel true
    And you could count on rain.

Yes, all was simply black or white.
    The present shades of gray
Are painted by a different hand
    For quite a different day.

The simple things of earth and sky
    Are lost to modern man,
For he must know the why and where
    And how it all began.

Call it progress if you will,
    Or scientific truth,
I'd rather things be as they were
    When I was in my youth.

185

BROTHERS

HE AND I WERE BROTHERS in a way;
And on those days when time, in leniency,
Offered us a respite from our work
We'd share in silence things that once had been
But are no more...

                  Treasures of the past:
Lilacs growing by a farmhouse door;
A hill behind, a field before, and cattle
Grazing down along the creek where cattails
Spread their summer snow; walnuts drying,
Laid out in the sun; empty cornstalks
Dying...
            Scenes that only memories know.

He'd often tilt his head as though to listen
To some far-off sound, his eyes would close,
And when they opened there would be a hint
Of mist...

            No need to speak. There were no words
We knew, for we were brothers in a way.

He and I were brothers in a way.

EVERGREEN
Corner

JUST ONE MORE TIME IS ALL I ASK:
   To climb the mountain trails again
   Where Cascades hold those two apart:
   The western shores and eastern plain:

   To taste the fruit of land and sea
   To hear the village chapel chime;
   To feel the fall's mist in my face;
   And feel that freshness one more time.

   Just one more time is all I ask.
   I've wondered far but now I fain
   Would travel back, to know the peace
   My childhood knew... to live again.

Excerpt: A CHRISTMAS DREAM
Wm. Spicer

Let me dream though dreams are vain,
Let me taste the time-worn lore,
Let me live it all again,
Let me be a child once more.

188

A Christmas Dream

WHEN THE CRISP, WHITE, CRUNCHY SNOW
  Covers tree and house and plain,
  And when Santa's "Ho, Ho, Ho"
  Echoes down the old back lane;
  When the gifts are wrapped and tied,
  Stockings stuffed with candy-cane.
  Vanity is set aside,
  Then I'm a child again.

  Time has made its presence known
  Youth has closed and locked the door.
  All too soon the years have flown...
  All too soon...and I implore:
  Let me dream though dreams are vain,
  Let me taste the time-worn lore;
  Let me live it all again,
  Let me be a child once more.

FOLIO TEN

LIVE →

About Today...

TAKE TIME TO LIVE →

—Now

FOLIO TEN

LIVE →

NATURE'S WAY
TAKE TIME
NOW
   QUOTE
...AND I
TURN IT OFF
AND SO...
   QUOTE
THE FOOL

Nature's Way

I DON'T NEED
THANKS FOR WHAT
I GIVE;
THE THANKS IS IN THE GIVING.
NATURE'S WAY IS "GIVE AND TAKE",
THE PERFECT LAW OF LIVING.

I CANNOT GIVE WITHOUT RETURN,
THE PRECEPT IS DIVINE.
THE BLISS IS IN GIVING, SINCE
THE NEED I FILL
IS MINE.

take time **TO LIVE**
take time **TO SHARE**
take time **TO PONDER**
TAKE
TIME **TO CARE**

Now...

NOW

With shutter speed we live, and leave
Our imprint on the film of time.
No future hope or past regret
Can ever make the print sublime

Tomorrow is an empty promise,
Always just a night away,
And yesterday a fading copy
Of the life we live today,

The image of a life is captured
In the time the gods allow,
And in the album of the ages
We shall live by living now.

You CAN Stack Silver dollars ALL THE WAY TO HEAVEN IF YOU CAN GET THE FIRST ONE ON the Level

...AND
I

He may have a million or so in the bank,
A nest egg or two on the side,
A chromium Stutz at his country estate,
A thoroughbred ready to ride.
He may have a yacht for a special occasion,
A girlfriend to quiver and sigh,
But he puts on his trousers one leg at a time
The same way that you do...and I.

She may have a box at the Opera Comique
While you and I wait in line,
A maid and a cook and a chauffeur..oh, yes,
She must have "before dinner" wine.
She buys and she buys whatever she wants,
Her money-well never goes dry,
But you know she puts on one shoe at a time
The same way that you do...and I.

I've always been short on material wealth,
It's pretty much "making ends meet".
I see how the rich live it "high on the hog"
And I think of "the bitter and sweet".
But live as they might there's an end for the rich,
Though they hope for a "sweet by-and-by",
They'll go to the graveyard as poor as a coot,
The same way that you will...and I.

197

TURN IT OFF

When your day is over
　　Turn it off.
So it wasn't clover
　　Turn it off.
Every day can't be your best,
Some are given as a test,
Your brains like muscles need to rest.
　　　　Turn it off.

Work a fair amount, then
　　　　Turn it off.
Give a square account, then
　　　　Turn it off.
No one knows how much you do,
No one cares what time you're through,
The only one who aches is you,
　　　　Turn it off.

If you're in a hurry
　　　　Turn it off.
If you tend to worry
　　　　Turn it off.
Take a little time to play,
Stop to bow — or kneel and pray,
Don't wait until you're old and gray,
　　　　Turn it off.

Take a little
time
to play,
stop to bow—
or kneel
& pray,
don't
wait until
you're old and gray
TURN IT OFF

Excerpt: TURN IT OFF
Wm Spicer

AND SO...

And so...with life, this grand performance
    More than half played out,
I ask, whatever is its purpose?
    What is life about?

"Why, life's for living," comes an answer.
    Well, I'd thought of that,
But isn't living also given
    To the dog and cat?

"Ah, yes," you say, "but we have brains
    With which to judge and plan."
Then show me ant or bee that cannot
    Out-produce a man.

And watch a robin build her nest,
    It's every bit an art.
She never wonders "how" or "why",
    She has no draft or chart.

And there's a dam the beaver built
    Of stones and logs and thatch.
And here a spider spun a trap
    No engineer could match.

Explain the Capistrano swallow
    And his built-in clock.
Then tell me which one was the teacher,
    The nightingale or Bach.

And so... I take a moment out
    To meditate and think
About the meaning of it all—
    To find the missing link.

I have a mind, there is a God;
    Of these I have no doubt.
But there remains that nagging question:
    What is life all about?

One wink is all I have It matters how, not where or why I face the brink of time and Jo I Live it now

THE FOOL

THE TREASURES OF THE WORLD ARE MINE,

I travel where I will
Across the sands of Africa
Or just beyond the hill
In restless moments I may scale
A jagged mountain peak
Or sail a sloop through Bengal Bay
Or on to Mozambique

I may prefer a Kashmir lakeside
With its' lotus bloom
The Kyber Pass may suit my fancy
Or Egyptian tomb
Or Buddhist temple in Tibet,
Or chapel in Seville...
The treasures of the earth are mine,
I visit them at will

You call me fool? A prisoner
Of mortar steel and glass?
You say there'll be no Kashmir lake
No sloop or Khyber Pass?
I see no walls, I see no prison
Life is what I think
And so I live in paradise
With books and pen and ink.

203

Part V

POETRY JUST FOR FUN

207

Life is what
I think
And so I live
In Paradise
With books and
Pen and ink.

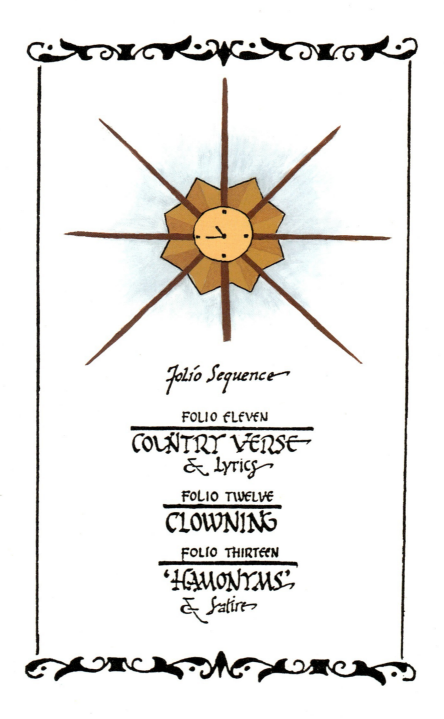

Folio Sequence

FOLIO ELEVEN
COUNTRY VERSE
& lyrics

FOLIO TWELVE
CLOWNING

FOLIO THIRTEEN
'HAMONYMS'
& satire

FOLIO ELEVEN

COUNTRY VERSE
& Lyrics

FOLIO ELEVEN

COUNTRY VERSE

FER RECITIN'
A DECLARATION
THE POET LAUREATE
SLIM PICKIN'S
THE BIBLE "BELT"
SPOOKIE SUE
SPRING FEVER

ADVICE T' PICKERS

— LYRICS —

I AIN'T MAKIN' WAR
MONA LIZ
A BALLAD OF THE SMOKIES
A BALLAD OF THE BUM

FER RECITIN'

My stuff ain't all that great, I 'spect.
    I try t' make it clear,
'N I jes' talk the same's I would
    If you was sittin' here.

'N if yer hank'rin' t' recitin'
    Some o' what you see,
You won't find nothin' fancy here,
    It's country jes' like me.

So make yerself feel right t' home,
    Jes' try a verse 'r two,
'N if you like the things I write,
    I'm much obliged t' you.

THE POET LAUREATE
A Favorite Fantasy

A TOUCH O' COUNTRY

JUNCTION'S
WHAT THEY CALL IT,
A PROMISE OF A PLACE.

A DECLARATION

Poet Laureate

O'

JUNCTION,
TENNESSEE

FER
The Twinkle 'N' Good Humor
O' Country Verse 'N' Lyrics
'N' The Likes O' That.
Nothin' Fancy.

215

'BOUT THIS HERE DECLARATION

The Poet LAUREATE

O' JUNCTION, TENNESSEE

I AM THE POET LAUREATE
  O' JUNCTION, TENNESSEE
I DON'T MIND SAYIN' I'M RIGHT PROUD
O' WHAT FOLKS DONE FER ME;
THE PEOPLE GATHERED IN THE SQUARE
AS FAR AS YOU COULD SEE,
AN' MADE ME POET LAUREATE
O' JUNCTION, TENNESSEE.

THEY HAD ME SING A SONG I WRIT,
'N THEN THE PARSON PRAYED,
'N THEN WE ATE THE VITTLES THAT
THE WOMANFOLK HAD MADE.
THEY READ A DECLARATION THERE
A-NEATH THE OLD OAK TREE
THAT MADE ME POET LAUREATE
O' JUNCTION, TENNESSEE

216

I PICK 'N SING THE ONLYEST THING
THAT THESE FOLKS WANT TO HEAR,
'N PEOPLE LIKE IT SO DURN GOOD
THEY COME FROM FAR 'N NEAR.
THEY SAY I AM THEIR PRIDE 'N JOY;
ON THIS THEY ALL AGREE,
I AM THE POET LAUREATE
O' JUNCTION, TENNESSEE.

THE FIDDLIN'S DID BY MAYOR BROWN
THE SAW BY WILLIE CASE,
THE BARBER PLAYS THE OL' MOUTH-HARP
'N DOUBLES ON THE BASS.
'N THEN THEY ALL PITCH IN 'N SING—
IT'S ALWAYS KEY OF "C".
I AM THE POET LAUREATE
O' JUNCTION, TENNESSEE.

I SPENT MY LIFE IN THESE HERE PARTS,
A-HUNTIN' IN THE WOOD;
I NEVER MET A LAUREATE,
I S'PECT IT'S SOMPIN' GOOD.
IT MAY NOT BE TOO PROPER, STILL,
I'M PROUD AS I CAN BE,
'CAUSE I'M THE POET LAUREATE
O' JUNCTION, TENNESSEE.

Slim PICKIN'S

I jes bin settin' here a-rockin',
   Thinkin' 'bout the day
   The Lord will come with all His host
   'N' take the saved away.

I can't help speculatin' some
   As who the saved will be,
   'N' hopin' when the sheep is picked
   That one o' them is me.

I guess I'd swap a patch o' peas
   I' be up there with Him,
   But if He takes the likes o' me,
   Well, pickin's must be slim.

Now take the reverend and his wife,
   why pshaw, they're boun' t' go;
   The ejucated way they talk
   'N' always dress jes' so.

'N' there be Charlie Bean, the miller
    Got the purtiest prayer.
    I 'spect he'll be a-prayin' when
    The roll is called up there.

There's Nellie Jones, she leads the singin',
    Teaches Sunday School,
    'N' always sees there's flowers in the
    Outer Vestibule.

I guess it's best that I ain't judgin';
    Everyone I see
    Has got some special kind o' goodness,
    'Ceptin' maybe me.

Now livin' that comes easy, jes' like
    Puttin' on your hat,
    But dyin', that's the kind o' thing
    I ain't had practice at.

There's one thing sure, I'm done with farmin'
    Future's mighty dim,
    'N' like I said, If He takes me
    Well, pickin's must be slim.

A
B
I
B
L
E

"
B
E
L
T
"

Ol' Noah built hisself a boat,
    Collected all worth countin',
Then rid the flood out high 'n' dry,
    'N' landed on a mountain.

They's folks what say they don't believe
    In nothin' they cain't see.
I read it in the Holy Word—
    That's good enough fer me.→

A whale he up 'n' swallered Jonah,
    Swum around awhile,
'N' coughed him up 'n' spit him out
    On some deserted isle.

They's some folks say it didn't happen,
    Things like that cain't be.
I read it in the Holy Word—
    That's good enough fer me→

Now Josh were fightin' Amorites,
    He had some more t' kill.
He didn't like t' work at night
    So had the sun stand still.

They's some what say the sun cain't stop,
    But I'll jes' guarantee
I read it in the Holy Word—
    That's good enough fer me—.

Daniel in the lion's den,
    He weren't a bit afraid.
Them lions purred like pussy cats,
    An' Daniel, he jes' prayed.

They's some what say it's jes' a story,
    Such a thing cain't be.
I read it in the Holy Word—
    That's good enough fer me—

They's them what claim the Bible's got
    Some things that they cain't go.
I mus' admit they's lots o' things
    I don't begin t' know.

But I'll keep readin' in that book,
    As long as I kin see,
An'—halleluiah! Praise the Lord—
    That's good enough fer me—.

SPOOKIE SUE

They call me Grandma Suzan, leastwise
To my face they do,
But other times when I cain't hear 'em
It's jes "Spookie Sue".

The reason is I got a knack
O' sorta prophesyin',
Like when sompin' bad's a comin'
'R when someone's dyin'.

When I hear a dog a-howlin',
    Sun-up 'r before,
I know there'll be some crepe a-hangin'
    On somebody's door

'N when that wind's a-moanin', Lowd,
    It's talkin right t' me,
T' let me know it's someone's time
    'N who that someone be.

I 'spect I heerd a hundred names,
    I seed 'em come 'n' go,
'N when the wind says it's that time
    You better bet it's so.

I always wondered if that voice
    Would someday prophesy
That Grandma Suzan's time had come
    That she was 'bout t' die.

Last night the south wind wailed a name
    I heerd me askin', "who?"

An' then so soft I scarce could hear,
    It whispered, "Spookie Sue".

SPRING FEVER

'Long about this time o'year
A feelin' takes a-hold
'N makes me wanta jes do nothin' —
Workin' leaves me cold;
Lest yer idee o' workin' be
A-layin' in the sun
'R wallerin' 'round here in the grass
'N not a-thinkin' none
'Bout nothin' 'ceptin' maybe fish
'R climbin' that thar hill
'R jes a-layin' back a-hearin'
That ol' whip-poor-will.

'course I know thar's work t' do;
I can't hep thinkin' though
That iffin I don't turn a hand
Them peas is gonna grow.
Them 'taters don't pay me no mind,
'N what's a coon 'r two?
Why shucks, them critters gotta eat
The same as me 'n you.

Jes' let me doze here 'neath this tree
Fer 'bout a month 'r so,
'N if they's crows down in the cornfield,
I don't need t' know.
When you come back, if I ain't breathin',
Don't you dare t' call;
Jes come up real quiet like
'N cheek my pulse, that's all.

ADVICE T' PICKERS

If yer inclined t' pick 'n' sing,
    I'll tell yeh what t' do:
Jes take down that ol' gitar there,
    'N git a friend 'r two,

Then run 'r through a couple times
    Until yeh feel the swing,
'N once yeh git 'r started good
    Yeh all pitch in 'n' sing.

So what if you don't know the tune.
    Why shucks, that ain't no trick,
This stuff will set itself t' music,
    You jes sing 'n' pick.

Lyrics

I AIN'T MAKIN' WAR

I had a gal in Tennessee,
As sweet as apple pie,
But Uncle had a job for me—
I kissed my gal goodby.

I kissed her by the garden gate,
I kissed her by the fence,
She promised me that she would wait
But I ain't seen her since.

CHORUS: Hey, Uncle Sam, don't point at me,
　　　　I bin that route before.
　　　　I don't mind makin' love. uh huh,
　　　　But I ain't makin' war.

I had a hog, I had a dog,
　　I had a milkin' cow,
I had a gal that I could love
　　But I ain't got one now.

I learned to shoot, I learned to s'lute,
　　I learned to hup-two-three.
They dressed me like a soldier boy
　　And shipped me over-sea.

CHORUS REPEAT

I got no grits or turnip-greens,
　　I got no apple pie,
But what I et you better bet
　　Would make a preacher lie.

I missed my hog, I missed my dog,
　　I missed ol' Tennessee,
But most of all I missed the gal
　　Who wasn't missin' me.

CHORUS REPEAT

MONA LIZ

My daughter is a purty thing,
 We call her Mona Liz.
She got her looks from Ma because
 Her daddy still has his.
Her hair is blonde, her eyes is blue,
 You'd know she is my kin
By way her nose is turned up and
 The dimple in her chin.

CHORUS: It's Mona Liz! Mona Liz!
 Where can that young 'un be?
 They's not another like her
 In the state of Tennessee

She's country style from head to toe,
 As fresh as new-mown hay;
She weaps a patch of nettles jes
 To keep the boys away.
When special doin's is in town
 Where young 'uns oughtn't be,
She saunters down the street and sings,
 "They ain't no flies on me."

232

CHORUS REPEAT

The last big blizzand that we got,
    Nigh half the town folk friz
A-waitin' in the snow to git
    A look at Mona Liz.

They's some folks think I zaggerate,
    But if I've told a lie,
The good Lord strike me dead right now...

233

A BALLAD OF THE SMOKIES

I've had my fill o' the city,
The buildin's row on row;
I've got my eye on a different sky
In the Smoky Mountains. So...

I'm off t' the hills, my darlin',
I'm off t' the hills, my dear;
I'm off with a pack an' a duffle sack,
An' I'm off with my fishin' gear.

I've done my time in the city,
A public no-man's-land.
I hear the call o' the mountains tall.
Yep, the waitin's over. An'...

I'll sing me a song o' freedom,
I'll sing me a song o' cheer;
I'll sing me a lay o' far away,
An' I'll sing it loud 'n' clear.

The call was long time a-comin',
My hair is turnin' gray,
But my voice is strong an' I know the song,
And I know jes' what t' say:

I'll git me a place in Georgia,
I'll git me a case o' rye,
I'll git me a hack an' a run-down shack,
An' I'll stay there till I die.

THE BALLAD OF THE BUM

I'm hikin' down the railroad track,
   A-lookin' fer a train.
I don't mind walkin' in the sun
   But I don't like the rain.
I got no home, I got no wife,
   I got no one t' care.
I'd take a coach t' Timbuktu
   But I ain't got the fare.

Wooo! Wooo! Hear that whistle,...
   Hear that whistle cry
I'm jes' a bum 'n I'll be one
   Until the day I die.

A cattle train went puffin' past,
   Ol' Casey rung the bell.
I said, "No, thank you, Mr. Jones,
   I jes don't like the smell."
He stuck his head out an' he yelled
   A "Well, how do you do,
I never pulled a cow that smelled
   Nigh half as bad as you."

Wooo! Wooo! Hear that whistle,...

236

I met a man the other night
    As I was beddin' down.
He climbed upon my haystack and
    He said, "My name is Brown."
I said, "Goodnight, I'd be obliged
    If you'd be on your way."
He said, "My man, I own this land,
    Yer sleepin' in my hay."

Wooo! Wooo! Hear that whistle . . .

I knocked upon a cottage door,
    I said, "Good mornin' mam,
I wonder, could you spare an egg
    An' jes' a slice o' ham?"
She said, "You chop that pile o' wood,
    I'll set the coffee perkin'."
I said, "No, thank you, Mrs. Smith,
    I jes' aint used t' working."

Wooo! Wooo! Hear that whistle!

CLOWNING

The Fun & Chuckles of
CLOWNING Around In Verse
& Light-Minded Buffoonery

FOLIO TWELVE

CLOWNING

FAREWELL TO SOCKS
ALLEGORICALLY SPEAKING

— CLOWNING WITH THE POET'S PEN —

CHEECHAKO OR SOURDOUGH
WHO YOU KIDDIN'?
DOWN WITH LIQUOR
ONE TOO MANY

"ON HOLD"

— LIGHT-MINDED BUFFOONERY —

WELL...I'LL BE DARNED
HEY! HEY! THE COUNTRY'S RUNNING
TELEVISION MADNESS

A Farewell to Socks

Farewell, oh socks, the time has come
 That you and I must part.
The happy hours that we have spent
 Will linger in my heart.

I must confess you have no holes,
 You do not itch or scratch.
Then why must I get rid of you?
 Because you do not match.

I ask you now, while one is brown,
 The other shades of gray —
Dare I be seen by foe or friend
 In such a mixed array?

I've tried to find some fault with each:
 Alas there isn't any,
And you will go where good socks go,
 And I to J.C. Penney.

ALLEGORICALLY SPEAKING

VERSES, like the human race,
    Of kinds are more than ample:
    Some are quite ridiculous,
    The following for example:

LIVES are much like posey patches,
    Laid with bulbs and seeds.
    It seems that some are blessed with blossoms,
    Others just get weeds.

A LOVE-AFFAIR is like a maze,
    With twist and turn and doubt.
    Its easy enough to get inside
    But just try getting out.

ROMANCE is like a budding rose,
    With beauty all-pervading.
    And, like the rose, the issue is
    To keep the thing from fading.

A WEDDING is a funeral,
    But whether corpse or vowers,
    The edge is with the wedded since
    They get to smell the flowers.

CLOWNING WITH THE POET'S PEN

NONSENSE GOOFY CAPERS   LIGHT-MINDED BUFFOONERY

FUN WITH JOKES

and gags and capers

The clowns need not rehearse

And when they jest with poets pen,

Their words come out in verse→

CHEECHAKO OR SOURDOUGH

You claim to have seen the grandest sights
This country has to show.
Since yours is such a liberal lore
There is something I would know:
Have you ever seen the Northern Lights
Across Alaskan sky,
Or female salmon fight their way
Back home to spawn and die?
Have you ever seen a midnight sun
That never needed set,
A Tlingit fishing through the ice,
Or Chilkat cast his net?

Have you ever seen a glacier calve
An iceberg with a roar
And watched the waters pitch and tumble
For a mile or more?
Have you ever seen the antics
Of an inebreated clooch,
Or shot a bear and sold his hide
For one big snort of hooch?
Well if you have, you've seen it all,
Your tag is "Sourdough",
But if you haven't, that's too bad,
You're still a "Cheechako".

WHO YOU KIDDIN'?

The cat said, "I'm a mean ol' dog."
    The dog said, "I'm a cat."
You know they both stayed what they were
    In spite of this and that;
A robin ain't no sandhill crane,
    A fly jes' ain't no bat.

The cat said, "I'm a fightin' fool,"
    And he was partly right.
That he was fool there ain't no doubt
    For what's a stranger sight
Than pussy-cat and ol' pit bull
    A-havin' them a fight?

Now here's a dog that thinks he ain't;
    He wants to be a kitten.
Fer him, an airedale mixed with shepherd
    Flea and hunger-bitten,
Cuddlin' on a lady's lap
    Is anything but fittin'.

My story has a moral to it:
    Beans ain't caviar.

Your part in life may be a "bit"
    Or you may be a star;
But don't be what you ain't, jes' be
    The best of what you are!

DOWN WITH LIQUOR

You say I am a HANDSOME Dude,
   The Valentino kind?
   I wouldn't disagree with that
   If I WAS so inclined.
   The mirror has a different tale,
   It says I'M old and fat
   But You say I'm a HANDSOME Dude;
   By George, I'll drink to that.
You say I Have a brilliant Mind,
   The PLATO type, you claim?
   THat may be just a little sTRong,
   Some folks that I could Name
   Would say that I am down-right dull,
   THat all I do is blat.
   But you say I am brilliant—And
   By George, I'll Drink to that.
So down with LIQUOR, keep 'er down,
   And fill 'er up again.
   We'll drink to the things we ARe
   And all the things we've been;
   We'll drink to "him", we'll Drink to "Her",
   We'll drink to Mike and Pat...
   You say I've had too much to Drink?
   By George I'll Drink to that!

246

ONE TOO MANY

She dabbed her face with powder and stuff;
She eyed her work with a croon;
She looked AT me and then I could see —
MY God! She had powdered a prune!

Her head rolled back like a woman half-dead;
I swear, it was something to see.
one of her eyes turned to the skies,
The other looked SQUARELY at me.

I grabbed my bottle, I ran for the door,
And there for a moment
I tarried;
And then I could see
That fateful decree
In her hand.
Good Lord!
we were Married!!!

"ON HOLD"

My back is ackin' an' my head
    Is givin' me a fit.
I'm 'fraid to walk, my leg is game,
    'Bout all I do is sit.

But when I sit fer very long
    My feet begin to swell,
My butt gets sore from sittin' here
    N' I jes' feel like HELL.

My hearin's gone, my eyes is weak
    I'm losin' all my hair;
I never have no company,
    Jes' me 'n' this ol' chair.

I git a pittance fer insurance
    From my Uncle Sam.
It's 'bout enough t' feed a mouse
    But I don't give a damm.

By gum, I'm only eighty-eight
    I put my life on "hold";
Imagine all the aches 'n' pains
    I'd have if I was old

— LIGHT-MINDED BUFFOONERY —

WELL...
I'LL BE DARNED

It seems like only yesterday
That you and I first met.
Engraved upon my memory,
I never shall forget
The sunshine of that day in June,
With magic in its ray —
It wasn't June? The month was March?
It poured down rain, you say?
    Well, I'll be darned!

It seems like only yesterday
That you and I were wed.
The chancel laid with floral sprays
Of white and green and red.
I see it now, the satin gown,
The train of apricot —
You say there was no train or gown?
A justice "tied the knot?"
    Well, I'll be darned!

250

There may have been no nuptial June,
No sacrament in style,
No "something borrowed, something new,"
Or walking down the aisle,
But you were lovely then as now,
A treat for eye to see.
And fortune smiled on me that day—
You say that you agree?
    Well, I'll be darned!

HEY, HEY! THE COUNTRY'S RUNNING

They wobble and they bobble,
They quiver and they quake;
The man who lives across the street,
The lady by the lake.

The girl who wears the skimpies,
The boy who has the dog,
They walk and run and jump and skip,
They sprint and race and jog.

They're puffing down the sidewalk,
They're sweating through the park.
I see them at the break of dawn
I hear them after dark.

Hey, hey! The country's running,
They'll keep the body fit.
But what about the mental part?
What shall they do for it?

The jogging man goes shopping,
He drives down to the store;
And hunts until he finds a place
To park, right by the door.

The lady with the bobbles,
She wobbles near and far;
But when she goes next door to chat
She has to take the car.

The girl in brief (I'm punning)
Has put on quite a fuss;
She has to walk a block to school
Because she missed the bus.

The boy with dog is pool-side,
His life is truly hard;
He stretches out and watches while
His mother mows the yard.

Hey, hey! The country's running!
The muscles bulge and swell.
Could it be true they're busy swapping
Brains for brawn? Ah well.

Television Madness

The camera was chasing a low-flying car
down a back-country stretch
I could see the driver was young and wore
goggles and black leather jacket,
the kind that you see on the "last lone survivor"
of some New York gang war. The car whirled
around with its' two headlights bugged like
the eyes of a creature from Mars
as I watched them they
turned into PIZZAS!
I heard myself asking "Is this
the main feature, a news break
or WHAT?

Now...
The camera was fixed on a girl
It was dark but a viewer could
see the over-tight jeans with the
factory patches, the blouse hanging
open and hair blowing free.
"Now that is a girl, I can tell."
(I confess that I talk to myself
quite a lot when I'm stuck to the
tube.... "What the HELL, she has just DISAPPEARED!"

254

THE PICTURE HAD CHANGED TO A BAR,
DONALD DUCK HAD BEEN HAVING A DRINK
AND I THINK THAT THE GUY WITH THE
GOGGLES AND JACKET WAS HAVING A BEER WITH
THE GIRL IN THE JEANS WHO WAS EATING A
PIZZA, I THOUGHT "WHAT WE NEED IS the
CAR TO APPEAR

THEN LIKE MAGIC THE
SETTING WAS CHANGED TO A CASTLE
SURROUNDED BY MOAT AND GUARDS STANDING stately
AND OUT CAME with his SWORD
the KING BRANDISHED HIGH!

AND HE SAID "Have you driven a Ford lately?"

FOLIO THIRTEEN

'HAMONYMS' & Satire

The Wit & Laughs of
'HAMONYMS' &
The 'Bite' of Satire

HOMONYMS
PLUS HAM

FOLIO THIRTEEN

'HAMONYMS'

(HOMONYMS PLUS HAM)
SIX SELECTED 'HAMonyms'
THE BORN AGAIN SINNER

THE 'BITE' OF SATIRE
WISDOM OF SILENCE
THE AWAKENING
INFLATION
INFINITE JUDGMENT
PATIENCE, MR. SMITH

'HAMONYMS'
— Homonyms Plus Ham —

The robin was hatching her eggs,
The father looked on with dismay;
"I say, am I Jekylled? These eggs are all speckled."
"Just a lark." And that's all she would say.

—◆—

The hunter was drunk as a lord,
He couldn't tell whisky from water.
A gal happened by, he gave her the eye,
She said she was game, so he shot her.

The Bureau of Indian Affairs
Has failed its genetic endeavor.
The siwash and crow, and others I know,
Have more affairs now than ever.

— ◆ —

"You're driving me crazy," he said.
And hers was a comparable cut;
I honestly fear you're bragging, my dear,
That's really no drive, that's a putt."

— ◆ —

Arrested for indecent exposure.
His counsel, always the shrewdest,
Had only to mention the defendant's contention,
You can't pin a thing on a nudist.

The measure of friendship is use,
With never allowance for bungle.
I offer in brief the cannibal chief
who passed his friend in the jungle.

The cannibal's choice was the clergy;
The catholic boiled on the fire.
with a shake of his head, the clergyman said,
"you'll never boil me. I'm a friar."

THE BORN AGAIN SINNER

I turned my back to the stained-glass ball,
    To the altar, the nave and the spire.
I stopped my ears to the story of heaven,
    And hell with its brimstone and fire.

I turned my face to the sea and sky,
    To the mountains the ages have wrought.
I opened my ears to the song of the bird,
    And that was the heaven I sought.

The 'Bite' of Satire

THE WISDOM OF SILENCE

THE SAGE WAS ASKED TO COMMENT ON
An issue of the state.
His reputation hung there — as
A life-span hangs on fate.
The listening audience waited, but
A sigh was all it heard;
The wise man turned and walked away;
He didn't say a word.

A POLITICIAN NOTED HOW
The stage was timely set.
He started speaking then and there;
I guess he's speaking yet.
I voted, and my vote to some
Would seam a bit absurd.
I voted for the speaker who
Had uttered not a word.

THE AWAKENING

"**I'm** SICK OF FARMING," SAID THE MAN,
"This wretched little place—!
I think I'll leave this country life
And join the human race.

HE SOLD HIS FARM AND MOVED AWAY.
He made his share of wealth.
But nothing comes without a price;
It cost him years and health.

HE SAID, "I'LL FIND A QUIET PLACE.
"I'm tired and I'm old."
He bought himself a little farm,
Just like the one he sold.

INFLATION

THERE ISN'T A DOUBT MECHANICS KNOW
JUST HOW TO BAIT A HOOK.
AND THEY CAN TELL WHEN THERE'S A SUCKER
READY TO BE 'TOOK'.

SUPPOSE, FOR EXAMPLE, A TIRE IS DOWN:
  "Your problem isn't air;
  The front-end alignment's out, you know,
  That caused the extra wear.

"THE TIRE ON THE OTHER SIDE IS 'GONE';
  The brakes should be replaced,
  The cylinder's leaking, shocks are bad,
  The 'what's it' isn't spaced,

"WHICH LIKELY ACCOUNTS FOR WHY THE BEARINGS
  Grind the way they do.
  Six-hundred and fifty bucks, I'd say,
  Will make her run like new."

NOW HE DOESN'T KNOW OR LIKELY CARE
  The car is new, you see.
  The job that he does, and does the best,
  He'll do on you and me.

SO NOW YOU'VE BEEN WARNED, THE TRUTH IS OUT,
  The truth about 'repair'.
  Don't pay for a major job, my friend,
  When all you need is air.

266

INFINITE JUDGMENT

IT WAS A SULTRY SORT OF DAY
  THAT SETTLED O'ER THE TOWN,
AND MANY A FARMER RAISED AN EYE
  BENEATH A WORRIED FROWN.

"OH GOD," SAID ONE. "PLEASE GIVE US RAIN:
  The crops are so in need;
  The creek is dry, the fields are parched,
  The cattle have no feed."

ANOTHER, KNEELING BY HIS BED,
  Declared in fervent prayer:
  "Thou knowest, Lord, that what I need
  Is weather dry and fair.
  My earthly goods in storage kept
  Would not survive a rain
  Until my weather-damaged roof
  Is shingled once again."

THE LORD LOOKED DOWN UPON THESE TWO
  Of equal justly cause,
  And thought, "How can I please them both
  With self-same set of laws?"
  He knew full-well to compromise
  Was not without a price.
  So, reaching forth His mighty hand,
  He rolled His heavenly dice.

"PATIENCE, MR. SMITH"

TH DAY IS STIFLING, HOT AND HUMID;
DID SOMEBODY SAY
THAT WINTER'S JUST AROUND THE BEND
AND SPRING NOT FAR AWAY?

Ho hum! It matters not
If I be prompt or late;
It's "Patience does it Mr. Smith"
And so I wait and wait.

MY EARS ARE BOMBED WITH GARBLED SOUNDS
THE MODERNS CALL IT 'ROCK';

JUST CLEAR THE AISLE AND WAIT AWHILE
AND YOU WILL GET YOUR BACH.

　　Ho hum! It matters not
　　If I be prompt or late;
　　It's "Mr. Smith, please take a seat
　　And wait..." and wait and wait.

I CAST MY LINE, I HEAR A VOICE,
AND GUESS WHAT I AM TOLD:
"ALL FISH ARE BUSY AT THE MOMENT,
WOULD YOU CARE TO HOLD?"

　　Ho hum! It matters not
　　If I be prompt or late;
　　It's "Take a number, Mr. Smith,
　　And wait..." and wait and wait.

IN DEATH COULD I BUT OCCUPY
MY HEAVENLY CHATEAU,
BUT "THERE'S NO ROOM RESERVED FOR SMITH
YOU'LL HAVE TO WAIT BELOW."

　　Ho hum! It matters not
　　If I be prompt or late;
　　It's "Things are rough here, Mr. Smith.
　　You'll have to wait and wait."

Part VI

FINALE

The Best
Is Yet
To Be
DONE

274

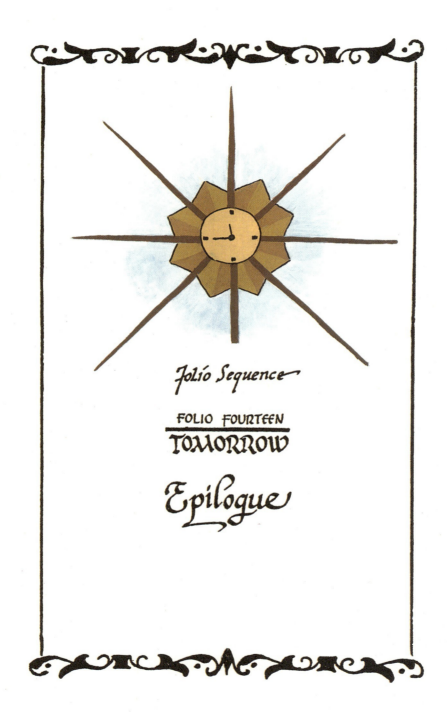

Folio Sequence

FOLIO FOURTEEN
TOMORROW

Epilogue

275

FOLIO FOURTEEN

TOMORROW

The Dawn of
TOMORROW

FOLIO FOURTEEN

FINALE

TOMORROW

IF I HAD TIME
THE WORLD IS WAITING
THE VERSE OF LIFE

▼▼▼

THE VERSE OF LIFE
— FINALE —
Epilogue

IF I HAD TIME

I'D FIX THE TRELLIS..
so the flowers
Would have a place to climb,

I'D LEARN TO PRAY..
and meditate
And think on things sublime.

I'D DO ALL THE THINGS
I ought to do...

IF I JUST HAD THE Time

Excerpt: IF I HAD TIME
Wm Spicer

279

IF I HAD TIME

IF I had time I'd fix the roof
　　Before another rain,
And give that door to Jimmy's room
　　Another coat of stain.
I'd fix the trellis so the flowers
　　Would have a place to climb,

And edge the grass along the walk...
 If I just had the time.
If I had time I'd go to church
 And learn about my soul.
I'd take communion, pay my tithe
 And practice self-control.
I'd learn to pray and meditate
 And think on things sublime.
I'd do the things I ought to do...
 If I just had the time.

Time's a Scrooge, a thief, a miser:
 Never gives enough.
You plan a project, like as not
 He'll leave you in the rough.
There's not a bit of use to start,
 You'll never get it done.
Old Time will stop you in your tracks
 Before you've half begun.
I closed my eyes and tried to find
 A word that rhymed with "ought,"
When suddenly my mind received
 A most revealing thought:
That I could finish all my tasks
 In less than half the time
That I have used procrastinating,
 Doodling here in rhyme.

BUT...

THE WORLD IS

waiting

THE
WORLD
IS

THE BEST · STORY · HASN'T · BEEN · WRITTEN,
The best song has yet to be sung.
You may ogle and "ah"
At Matisse and Renoir
But the best painting hasn't been hung.

THE · BEST · POEM · HASN'T · BEEN · PRINTED,
The best book has never been read.
And in spite of the preachers,
The statesmen and teachers
The best words have yet to be said.

SO · FASTEN · YOUR · CART · TO · A · SUNBEAM,
And aim for the highest and best.
Give your all — and to spare
To the human share,
Then let go and let God do the rest.

Life is what I think and so I live in paradise With books and pen and ink

"God is a fancy, tho' fool sighted

The Inspiration of COURAGE & Commitment to Striving

I'd never heard a flower speak But this one did I swear.

The PEACE that I has sought —without was there

NATURE always hides her best

THE WONDERMENT OF NATURE & HER MASTERPIECES It is no disgrace to lose the race if you will give your best. Where,

I've Lost A Dream

The door to beauty is the soul; the poet holds the key

In all this sacred word, Did he say I must die?

THE PAIN OF PROGRESS — the colors of may

these gentlemen, by hardship tempered, WOULD NOT BEND THE KNEE TO DESPOT KING OR PRINCE OR LORD BUT CRIED OUT, "WE ARE FREE!"

THE TREASURES OF THE WORLD ARE MINE

Be careful what you dream about, A dream is often truth

He breathed the air of the fir and pine.

there is a torch that I can light

"There must be a God," the wise man said.

Memories

—don't mind who ballyhoo it—if you've

The Enchantment of DREAMS & Fantasies

I would spend hat is left in the hills of God

The Enrichment of BELIEVING & The Fulfillment

The Dawn of TOMORROW

LOVE

CHALLENGE FATE?

The Best Is Yet TO BE DONE

don't curse the clock that wakens you, —if you're the one who set it.—

What has become of the beauty I knew

The Verse of Life

When the verse of life has ended
And its being fades away,
Will my words all be forgotten
Or will there be those who say,
"I remember, they were worthy;
They were meaningful and clear"?
When the verse of life has ended,
Will they know that I was here?

When the final curtain closes
And the house is dark and still,
And my voice is somewhere speaking
On another stage and bill;
When I look back to the present
From the new-found life and sphere,
Dare I hope that in the silence,
They remember I was here?

Will I hear one voice declaring,
"He was here, yes, he was here"?

285

WILL MY WORDS ALL BE
fiorgotten?..

When the

Verge of Life

has ended
and it's being fades away

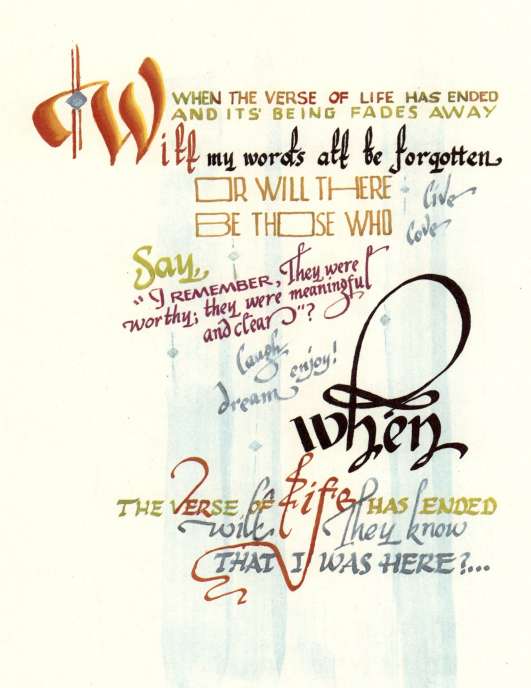

When the verse of life has ended
and its' being fades away
Will my words all be forgotten
Or will there
be those who
live
love
Say,
" I remember, They were
worthy; they were meaningful
and clear "?
laugh   enjoy!
dream
when
the verse of life has ended
will they know
that I was here?...

288

When
the FINAL CURTAIN closes
and the house is dark and still
And my Voice
is somewhere speaking
on another
Stage and
bill;
when
I look back to the
Present from the life and
NEW-FOUND SPHERE...

dare
I
hope...

... that in the silence
they remember I was here?

Laugh love
sing play
dream
live Enjoy
strive
believe
pray

Will I hear one voice

declaring

"He was here, yes, he was here"?

THE END

Epilogue

DON'T THANK ME...

For the poems I write;
   You see the thanks are mine
For verses grow in a poet's heart
   Like melons on a vine.

— William Spicer

DON'T THANK ME...

For my efforts.
 To present anothers dream, indeed,
The joy I hope it brings to you
 Is all the thanks I need.

Edith Reed

Index

303

Index to Excerpt & Quotes

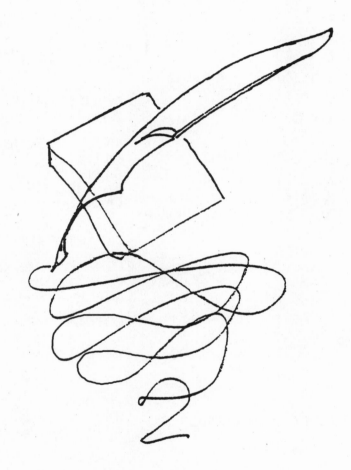

306